The Pocket Mirror

D0813436

Also by Janet Frame

THE POCKET MIRROR

POEMS BY

Janet Frame

GEORGE BRAZILLER / *New York*

Copyright © 1967 by Janet Frame
All rights in this book are reserved.
For information address the publisher:
George Braziller, Inc.
60 Madison Avenue
New York, N.Y. 10010
Library of Congress Catalog Card Number: 67-18210
ISBN 0-8076-1272-3

Printed in the United States of America

First paperback reprint edition, September 1991

The Pocket Mirror

Dunedin Poem

Here I've gone down with the sun
written syllables till time has surprised me
with the fact of his consistency.
I love not you but the sun's going down
so easily.

Soon will the days be dark? Will the mists come,
the rain blow from Signal Hill down Northeast Valley
that in winter lies in shadow?
I never remember the sun, in Northeast Valley.

The tramlines are torn from their sockets.
Things do not suffer as we supposed.
People suffer more than we supposed.
The buses tread softly, jerk to a stop, the doors slide open.
I climb in, traveling to where
down a long street lined with flowering cherry trees I walked
nineteen years ago
to stare at the waves on St. Clair beach.

The Clock Tower

I have settled now in my flat.
I have arranged my favorite books on the bookshelf.
I have moved the table for working in privacy and light.

There's a ripe grape-colored cherry tree,
a bed of geraniums,
a woman walking in white shoes, white gloves, white hat.

A sea gull circles the clock tower. His funereal white wings recall
pieces of old tombstone flying
when the wind strikes at the grave of a sea city.

1

Fog clouds drift on the hill.
Who lives, like an angel, in the clock tower?
The summer heat treads the color from the cherry tree.
The gracious cultural burden of the View,
the long-faced clean houses that claim their natural right
to hold students, books, to have high ceilings, white walls, neat
        flower beds,
will soon, I think, send my journeying memory into collapse.
Tomorrow I may be saying, "There are no slums in St. Kilda.
Hillside Road, the Workshops, Kensington are dreams.
I never lived in Playfair Street, Caversham, with my bedroom
        a linen cupboard,
or waited on a Saturday night party at the Grand Hotel,
or tried to resist the pleas of my hangwomen workmates.
              —You
need pearls.
Pearls take away that bare look from the neck.

Swans whose necks are bare
float on the Water of Leith.
The wind is south.
The century is late.

Six o'clock wine flows from the cherry tree.
Children go barefoot.
Men and women make promises.
None know, few care
who lives like an angel in the clock tower.

Speke Philip Sparrow, Speke

How simple it is in the night and the first light
when the sun is new on the leaves
melting the honeydew.

How clear the cottage with the white doorstep
white as salt
where somebody cried and went away like the tide
as the cobbler has gone away
("tic-tac-toe no more" nor sheet webbed nor candle)
and the frog in the well
and yesterday
an heap gramercy.

The cherry tree shines
with pink and red wines.
Soap-new people come and go
washing away the stale times' flow
in an heap to eternity
with the tramcars and the tramlines.
O the waste, the time unstained, shifted in a week!
Pretty in the glacier your stiff white feathers,
an heap gramercy.
Speke Philip Sparrow, Speke!

Sunday Afternoon at Two O'Clock

Downstairs a sweeping broom goes knock-knock-knock
in the corners getting rid of last week's dust.
The weather hasn't decided to rain or shine.
Downstairs the washing is hung out, brought in, hung out again
on the clothesline.

Having been to church the people are good, quiet,
with sober drops at the end of their cold Dunedin noses,
with polite old-fashioned sentences like Pass the Cruet,
and, later, attentive glorying in each other's roses.

3

The wind combs the sea gulls, like dandruff, out of the sky.
They settle, flaked small, on stone shoulder and steeple,
a city coastal infection without remedy.
Their scattered sea-hungry flocks disturb the good people.

Long past is Sunday dinner and its begpardons.
Cars start in the street. The ice-cream shop is open.
The brass band gets ready to play in the Botanical Gardens.
The beach, the pictures, the stock-car racing tracks beckon.

Seizing the time from the University clock, the wind
suddenly cannot carry its burden of chiming sound.
The waves ride in, tumultuous, breaking gustily out of tune,
burying
            two o'clock on Sunday afternoon.

A Resolution

People, heated to the brittle stage,
when dropped in cold water, crack.
I'll smile no more.
Milk, laundry, dust bin.
Sweet people, sweet smiling.
There's no time for this leisurely meal of late afternoon.
Milk, laundry, dust bin.
Yes, yes thank you, I'll smile no more.
I came here to write stories and poems,
not to cook peanut candy.
Darkness comes, with the sun gone down
over milk, laundry, dust bin.

I'll smile no more.
I came here to write.
Grim, absorbed, sane,
I'll stir the syllables
in the provided saucepan;

I'll sleep on the innerspring mattress,
I'll turn the key,
pay the rent,
spread protective newspaper,
sweep with the carpet sweeper,
but smiling no more I'll frown, frown,
(milk, laundry, dust bin)
as I write my stories down down
to their seabed in caves of stone.

I Must Go Down to the Seas Again

I must go down to the seas again
to find where I
buried the hatchet with Yesterday.

Big Bill

Big Bill, Big Bill, High School Boy, Accountant,
Cricket star, hero of Plunket Shield Play,
thirteen years ago I went to your wedding
at St. Kilda on a cold dark winter's day.

What happened between then and now, Big Bill,
to bring madness, murder, suicide your way,
riding with us in triple nightmare to your funeral
at St. Kilda on this cold dark winter's day?

"It was all over so soon in the neat suburban street
with the faded flowers in the garden.
The time of firing, the number of shots, the angle of the bullets
are not relevant for long,
but love and dread are: love and dread stay.

Others may have the pleasure and curse of them now; not I.
No one will want to own me or bury me. Much wrangling,
cross-questioning, witnessing, will wear the time away
as I go in triple nightmare to my funeral
at St. Kilda on this cold dark winter's day."

The New Building

In the new building the voices knock
like stones against the walls.
The partitions are thin.
The new building has a delicate inner skin
plastered with bookshelves to keep the sound in,
sound or wound. Trees planted in a hurry
droop in the courtyard among level pools
piped with clear water. Beds of grass are beginning
to get the architect's idea.
Swampy comes and goes
with fist of fog, storm, metallic light gonging
behind those whale-gray heavy clouds
whose blubber's in the heads of those
who can't think where the silence, like the money, goes,
once it's out of the soul and into the purse.

Yet I suppose things could be worse.
The hanging stairway in the library may well see
some interesting executions. The inner courtyard
is a surprise worth meeting; even under the leer
of Swampy's looming face the grass is trying,
the trees may recover,
the windows and the people may grow used to the glare
of the sun's rude stare;
and by and by
even I may mellow
into a busily writing Burns Fellow!

Sunday Morning

Salt water is poetry.
I did not decide this
or prepare a statement
to astonish; it is always

my pleasure on Sundays
looking out of my window
at the petal-white Dunedin light
to trace the green stalk

to its roots in the sea,
then say as the tentacles
take hold and I drown,
the oxygen of silence withheld—

salt water is poetry
not mine but the providers
whom I thank by reading
and wish never again to breathe the silent air.

Dunedin Morning

The Leith is always a loud grumbler
after a feed of high-country rain
and cannot keep its wide apron clean.

Smoke is early, earliest.
Birds wake, test gear, rest,
make a more subdued start upmorning.

On the city's doorstep, light,
diluted with last night's rain,
is taken in, opened, and seen

to be morning below the usual level of sun.
Cars, motorcycles, people start to complain.
Wise Swampy wears well-bred cony on her shoulder.

Down comes the rain; and later,
in the city of the Globe, the Playhouse and His Majesty's Theater,
with an expert change of scene, the noon sun.

Mountaineer

What do they know of John Keats
who only John Keats know?
The lecturer in his office sits
grinding a mountain to snow,
saying I only know
John Keats and I are humble men.
My boots walk in the snow,
his noble words they go
on bare rock and wild cliff-face
to teach me it is true
eternity doth tease our thought,
our death is long our breath is short,
our life comes not again.
John Keats and I are humble men
but his words among the snow
have more than ease my thoughts to tease
while my boots hurt so!

Leith Street

From black-edged matchbox buds
the elms have shaken out
their silk handkerchief leaves,

promising fire later; green
waving streamers glossy ribbons,
what do they mean why must they mean,
we'll not go satisfied
unless there is explaining:
at ear level the gift is pearl-drop;
to be and mean and stand in spring leaf
is triply possible; sun
brushes a leaf; what gilt; what guilt
turns the spring highway to stone;
as out of the wax vestas the melting virgins come,
blossom and burn; oh no,
this is an innocent birthday party where magicians
dazzle with silk handkerchiefs and snow,
think rabbits, live their habits,
and never know, never know.

Chant

Down with summer spring autumn winter,
give me deep freeze for ever,
icicles on roofs walls windows the allwhite
alltime allover dream of a world and its people frozen
within the blackest night, so black it's impossible to discern
the alltime allover allwhite dream.

Now blind eyes come into their own.

Morning

Morning rain
decided early so people going
to work may take umbrella coat

may fairly share in earliest knowing;
morning with a clear vote a cool mind
has chosen rain with gusts of cold wind.

No false promise unnatural
six o'clock shine of sun on spring
blossom but murky light dull
dark sky, no "flattering mountaintop"
but rain raining downdrop nonstop

and only fools complaining.

Views

1

The poplars march down in flame
to Dunedin
as to a new Dunsinane.

The old generals polish their armor.
Macbeths cowering in the city
see ghosts rise in the vacant places,
crones and trees
working wand in leaf with prophecies.

2

A tall poplar
stands a brown blur of leaf-scribble and shading
with an aristocratic white house glimpsed through it
like the entrails of an X-ray painting.

3

Round heads of soft green bush
or cockabully brown with flat speckled heads
half-dark in shadow
draw the heart out, like mother earth,
to fondle their shape, to fight,
jealous of the wet nurse of sunlight.

4

Sea gulls alone, rarely alone, look like doves,
feast on honey and fresh air.

Back to the flock.
Give me my unfair share
or my beak draws blood:
This is total war.

The Place

The place where the floured hens
sat laying their breakfast eggs,
frying their bacon-colored combs in the sun
is gone.

You know the place—
in the hawthorn hedge
by the wattle tree
by the railway line.

I do not remember these things
—they remember me,
not as child or woman but as their last excuse
to stay, not wholly to die.

Thistledown

Thistledown with its white spider-spokes
tests my windowpane—
i happened to pass
i'm looking in
this thing that is between us
is glass

i'm off now
can't stay
can't rest
away away
to break my white prick in
a dark lady's nest.

Season

There is nothing to be done
no stone of surprise to unturn
no leaf to start from the bare tree
no ripple to be born on the pond that is iced over
no bud to burst into flower
seedling weed to trespass
sun to visit and stay till a late hour
for the year at the locked iron gate has stopped dead.
Winter is here
summer is gone
there is nothing to be done.

Sunday Drive

A dialogue is not the best way
to contain and capture last Sunday
yet we were two that, unlike the sea gulls, spoke words.

"Terns churr-churr. That is their sound," you said. "Sea swallows
birds with graceful flight diving and soaring like fish in air.
Their tails are like fishes' tails too."

Under the trees the puppet daffodils shook their heads
nodding agreement to a plan we knew nothing of. Their applause,
                    approval,
guided by the wind, continued
after we were gone while the dark trees above rocked
slowly, solemn breves to the golden demi-semi-quaver tune.
I thought their heads would be shaken off and roll downhill
into the green valley. It was hard to believe that on a still day
the daffodils stood with heads bowed
in gold shock under their yolk of calm.
You said as you started the car and drove away,
"There may be only a week left in which to see them.
They will be dead soon."

Dead, over, gone. How we accept it, in flowers!
We come in season to stare and go away murmuring,
"The show is better than ever this year."

Around the bay the waves were dark, crested with white,
like creatures moving alive under a wide blue blanket
with nobody warning them, Keep still!
Small waves trying to climb too high to see over the heads of those
                    in front,
dark periwinkle waves, blue-skirted above a funnel of snow
with the wind sucking the honey of sound through.
Wallflowers along the clay bank, taking a warm glowing hold
with suncolor and smell and (more practical)
with summer root, velvet cloaks wound
buttoned against the inquisitive wind.

And then at the bach around the bay
we stopped to rest and eat and talk
and imagine the city hills misted with dark virgin bush
before you and I and we and they and they came.

We knew how the land appeared then. We remembered
as we remember clearly the world before birth
when waterfalls touched our skin and we grew, thinking, first
we might be a tree or tadpole until the oppression of knowing
surged in us refusing to set us free
from what we had begun to be.
Now only parts of us, like our thoughts, glow, are glossed with
sun and fall
brittle in shapes of dust
as leaves do, giddy leaves growing first on a green tree.

Sheltered from the sea wind we lazed and looked.
You chuffed a lawnmower over the grass
then served lemonade and crushed orange, measuring fair levels
in bottle and cup as if it were childhood we had driven back to.
"My favorite toy," you said, "was a tea set
kept out of reach, not belonging to me, of blue enamel; I thought
my heart would burst in its beating when I was allowed to pour out
tea from the tiny blue teapot with the question-mark spout.
And what was your favorite toy?"

"Mine," I said, "was a kerosene tin. I dragged it along in the gray
dust
on a piece of string. It was shining and silver and hollow and it
sang in the sun
and everything that touched it made it sing exclaim groan tingle
cling-clang, gasp a tin gasp, and proclaim
its sound and shape and glossy being
as an empty new kerosene tin that sang and mirrored the world."

"Everything is always changing," you said.
"A tree does not want to be anything but a tree.
Hands are better than wings; hands can fly.
Everything changes. The dead clematis on that tree is a burden
to it.
It's like an old man with a sack on his back leaning towards the
sea.

Hear the waves?"

I quoted,
"Palpitation de la mer." A pulse beat.

"I would fight," you said suddenly, "if I were a child and my toys
        were taken away.
Would you fight?"

"As a child" I said, "I had few toys, no favorites. I cared most
for beetles and spiders, small cold creatures that lay
under stones, without sun."

"How lovely the periwinkle loops along the crisscross wire fence!
And the primrose flowering in the middle of the path. It was out
when we came here last. It is not dead yet.
Honeysuckle grows here.
There are four shelves of books in the sitting room. Poetry, the
        Old Testament.
I should like to stay here in winter, in the wild weather."

"Would it not be too cold?"

"I should like to stay here when storms come out of the sea, and
        frostferns work
their stiff embroidery on the windowpanes."

"Do you keep a diary?"
"I used to. I burned it. Do you keep one?"
"I do. Details I want to remember. Colors. A chance remark.
        A shape."
"My diary, years ago, was of love; of smiles given
near and far away as the sun; of passionate beings
out of reach but shining faithfully, like planets."

"Everything changes. Nothing will stay. My mother died four
        years ago,
and though I still do not mourn for her, I remember her.
Memory recurs, cripples. There is no relief from its pain."

"There is no measurement of time."

15

"Our parents are our first world. Do you remember
the childhood imagining of their death, of how it would be
with mother and father dead? How cruel winds came in
to take up the space they left, how exposed you stood
as on a headland, and could not bear the grief flowing
down down through your body to draw you into the earth?"

"I had no imagining of it. My mind and heart would not let me
see it.
I closed myself against it like a flower closing against the night."

"I saw it. Skipping,
Two little girls in navy blue
these are the actions they must do:
salute to the King,
bow to the Queen—
I would stop suddenly because my mother and father were dead
and there was no one above me to bend over me, there was nothing
above me save the sky.
Underchild, underdog, so happily under, and no one now to
intercept
the hawk, the bogie, the charging bull, the glass words of people,
their hooked faces and their wire smiles,
their stiff goemetric frowns."

"No, I never saw it. I would not let myself see it. When the
thought came
I made myself small and hid under a nasturtium leaf
and looked up, full of wise cunning, at the thin green rafters.
Oh, all is changing. All is different. Yesterday, today. Hear the
terns?
Their cry is always churr-churr-churr,
the repetitive deadening sentence;
but our words are not numbered; in crowds they come and go;
how I wish the few chosen would stay near,
close about us like threaded beads,
restricted like the cry of the tern!

"The day dazzles but is cold. Let us go home now.
It was like this and this and now it is not."
"When people are toys you cannot fight to regain them.
They are gone. Let us put our perplexity and pain
in the sack of dead clematis that the old man tree
swings
        towards
                the sea."

Museum Piece

The two-legged conduit
the white-haired pundit
the brown-eyed pond
the green-eyed wand
the white-faced lily
the red-haired holly
no longer feel the wrath
of the two-toed sloth.

A Poem

There is a poem like a young willow
in the first days of spring, a thread
of green sago on a bead-string,
but certain, predetermined
as the numbered chromosomes
that sway unshattered by
the furious undercurrent of heredity.

There is a poem vanishing like a kite-tail
high in the sky; concealing,

like darning wool,
the hole in Achilles' heel;
parceling with string
the birthday present and the clothes left behind
salt-filled, in the crib after the summer holiday.

There is a poem, a shape
of beads, bells or chains
not yet worn, rung nor imprisoning, but waiting
till the season of words comes round again
and the fruit is ripe and the cider golden
and the drunken poet starts to sing.

Question

Wayward as dust when the wind blows around corners
into blind eyes; petrifying as stone
that sinks the heart of thistledown.
Grave as gravity denied
supremacy in outer space,
tall metaphor, explain me,
describe my shape.

Instructions for Bombing with Napalm

naphthalene coconut oil
health
a neat lethal plan
a late net
an alp at panther heap
a pale ten-pin heel lent to plant help
to pelt
at nether halt
at nether halt
hell

concoct ointment
ultimate oil
unction
lotion
count coil
act lout to that tune in loin
toil out then
lick the lion's lap
cut the lint
pal

Story

farmers farming
sun sunning
rain raining
gunners gunning
pain paining
palms napalming
dollars doling
harmers harming
farmers farming

consuls consoling
peace piecing
treaties entreating
tills tolling
dollars doling
night knighting
gunners gunning
day delaying
sun sunning

gunners paining
consuls napalming

rain gunning
farmers entreating
night farming
day harming
dollars raining
peace delaying
sun tolling

O Lunq Flowerinq Like a Tree

O lung flowering like a tree
a shadowy bird bothers thee
a strange bird that will not fly away
or sing at break of day and evening.

I will take my knife
I will cut the branch of the tree
he clings to and will not let go
then the wide sky can look in
and light lay gloss
on the leaves of blood beating with life.

Oh yes, tomorrow I will take my knife
and the light and I will look in,
O plagued lung flowering like a tree,
said the surgeon.

The Whelk

The whelk in his shell
growing too cool
crept out in the sun and lying
there as in an oven
was soon cooked and eaten whelk-whole.

It was not man nor woman
drawn from man, was without blood bone or soul
yet as kindred without shell
it stole my compassion.

The Sun Shines All Day Vulgarly

The sun shines all day vulgarly
hurling gold nuggets at you and me,
burning our skin's privacy
our last poor wall and boundary.
If you love the common sun, they said,
your guilt will strike you dead.

But love the cherry tree in bloom
that holds no breath of greed or crime
that is purified light in a white room
and you will never come to harm.
They spoke as if eternity
had touched the cherry tree.

None told me that the sun would stay,
the cherry blossom wither and die,
and when its bloom was shed, the tree
cast off its guise of purity,
embrace light in its common mood
—wear a dark dress of blood.

Yet Another Poem About a Dying Child

Poets and parents say he cannot die
so young, so tied to trees and stars.
Their word across his mouth obscures

and cures his murmuring good-bye.
He babbles, *they say*, of spring flowers,

who for six months has lain
his flesh at a touch bruised violet,
his face pale, his hate clearer
than milky love that would smooth over
the pebbles of diseased bone.

Pain spangles him like the sun,
He cries and cannot say why.
His blood blossoms like a pear tree.
He does not want to eat or keep
its ugly windfall fruit.

He does not want to spend or share
the engraved penny of light
that birth put in his hand
telling him to hold it tight.
Will parents and poets not understand?

He must sleep, rocking the web of pain
till the kind furred spider will come
with the night-lamp eyes and soft tread
to wrap him warm and carry him home
to a dark place, and eat him.

At Evans Street

I came one day upon a cream-painted wooden house
with a white bargeboard, a red roof, two gates,
two kinds of japonica bushes, one gooseberry bush,
one apple tree lately in blossom; and thus I counted
my fortune in gates and flowers, even in the white
bargeboard and the fallen roofbeam crying religiously to the
                carpenter,
Raise me high! and in this part of the city that would be
high indeed for here my head is level with hills and sky.

It is not unusual to want somewhere to live but the impulse
bears thinking about seriously and it is wise
never to forget the permanent impermanence of the grave,
its clay floor, the molten center of the earth, its untiled
roof, the rain and sunbeams arrowing through slit
windows and doors too narrow to escape through,
locked by the remote control of death-bed convulsions
in a warm room in a cream-painted wooden house with
a red roof, a white bargeboard, fallen roofbeam . . .
                              no, it is not unusual
to nest at my time of year and life only it is wisest
to keep the spare room always for that unexpected guest, mortality,
whose tall stories, growing taller, tell
of the sea gull dwelling on bare cliffs, of eagles high
where the bailiff mountain wind removes all furniture (had eagles
                    known the need
for chairs by the fireside—what fire but the sun?) and strips the
                    hangings
from the trees; and the men, also, camouflaged as trees, who climb
                    the rock
face and of the skylark
from whose frenzied point of view harvest is hurricane
and when
except in the world of men
did hurricanes provide shelter and food?

In my house I eat bread and wish the guest would go.

The Clown

His face is streaked with prepared tears.
I, with others, applaud him, knowing it
is fashionable to approve when a clown cries
and to disapprove when a persistent sourface
does whether or not his tears are paint.

It is also fashionable, between wars,
to say that hate is love and love is hate,
to make out everything is more complex than we dreamed
and then to say we did not dream it,
we knew it all along and are wise.

Dear crying clown dear childlike old man
dear kind murderer dear innocent guilty
dear simplicity I hate you for making me pretend
there are several worlds to one truth when
I know, I know there are not. Dear people like you and me
whose breaths are bad, who sleep in and rumble
their bowels and control it until
they get home into the empty house or among the family
dear family, dear lonely man in a torn world of nobody,
is it for this waste that we have hoarded words over so many
million years since the first sigh, groan,
and look up at the stars. Oh oh the sky is too wide to sleep under!

Vacant Possession

All day on the phone. All day
desperate for vacant possession,
ringing to find if the furniture has gone
have I moved it yet; if not, why?

How can I explain
that my dead mother's best bedroom and fireside suite
have first claim, that their obstinate
will is to remain. Proud beasts they stand.
Nothing will shift them out
but the voice my mother used when she spoke to her
companionable furniture.

Now her voice is gone and the house is sold and I do not know
the command that persuades a well-loved fireside suite
meekly to rise up on its casters and go!

The Tree

There's a tree that's going to be cut down any day
and does not know it, for trees never know
until the axe-ripe time descends to sever their roots
from the cool underground pantry, earth-lined,
sun- and rain-supplied.
                              This one tree I have in view and mind
crowds a quarter of my window, waves finger-shaped branches
like a sea creature exploring, sensing in the blue surrounding
                    swirl and stir
encounters of pleasure and danger.

"Ugly old tree," I heard someone say.
"No one lives in the house now, anyway."
And soon, I know, the neighborhood will take up the cry.
"The tree is too old, too high
and all who lived in the house are dead or gone away."

It cannot keep still. Hour by hour
I have watched it and even when there's no wind blowing,
its whole being is astir: branches colliding, brushing leaf-tips,
evading one another, helplessly rocking to and fro
in the overpowering entirety
of a tree's night and day and night and day;
and it is only the watcher who grows weary.

Motels wait to be born: a new progeny, tastefully walled
with wisteria and clematis; an arterial rose
bubbles as a rare sign of life in the old garden.
I wanted to pick it but I decided not to.

It will stain the great axe when it comes riding by
knight-errant to rescue the suburban neighborhood
from the dangers of the view-encroaching tree
cradlerocking too sky-high and wild, senselessly
alive in a world where it is far more tactful
to feign death too many years before you die.

The Garden

Japonica petals like yellow crumbs
and red japonica with waxed petals;
hedgehogs snuffling and in the road
outside a dead hedgehog and its blood
like fuchsia petals.

I chopped off the heads of the grass. I had
a clear memory of what was lost—
the glittering spectacle of morning,
of grass going to the opera at the wrong time
beyond reason yet in rime and rhyme.

Furious in the delicate vulnerable
garden what else could I do?
I had to make it mine,
to eat the yellow crumbs scattered among
the leaves as if I had been
a bird in winter, to kill the common
green grass that willfully put on its crown
jewels in the morning.

Then my unease was gone,
I thought my battle for possession won.
I reckoned without the overworld sun
that burgling every strong-room

holds, keeps man, woman, house, garden,
to drop all one night
in the well
without a ripple.

Rain on the Roof

My nephew sleeping in a basement room
has put a sheet of iron outside his window
to recapture the sound of rain falling on the roof.

I do not say to him, The heart has its own comfort for grief.
A sheet of iron repairs roofs only. As yet unhurt by the demand
that change and difference never show, he is still able
to mend damages by creating the loved rain-sound
he thinks he knew in early childhood.

Nor do I say, In the traveling life of loss
iron is a burden, that one day he must find
within himself in total darkness and silence
the iron that will hold not only the lost sound of the rain
but the sun, the voices of the dead, and all else that has gone.

Napalm

nay
  son
    say
      psalm

pay
  palm
    sun
      day.

Crusts

Crusts upper and lower
brown and white
turn destruction
                into light
crack the sun
                that cracked the wheat
feed the people in famine street.

Photos

photos speed
to the heap of shot dead

host faces
cast in deep shade
hatch hope to stop
the sad pose

O the cost
of the deed of the dead past!

A Life Sentence

is
life
still

tense faces
cleft fin
faeces
feet lent
sentient

flee fail
fall fell
all
fast lance
act
final cell
infant scent
nest

call clan
listen feel
taste tell
is
life
still

Cherry Tree

Crowned white
at the door of light.
Tomorrow in sacrificial mood
kneeling in blood.
O cherry tree, the hand
of the green world wounds thee.

Said the grass, I embraced your white blossom.
Now shelter me, dark-leaved artery
beating against the sky.
I am fur on the skin of the earth,
I am graves and volcanoes
clay and fire in winter dress.

You, cherry tree,
with your lost white joy

stem like a wounded limb
from my green body,
yet no man whose hand bleeds
has birds fly there to sing to him.

Green and red
share wine and blood,
the cherry tree wounded and wed,
the green grass growing
for the mowers' mowing
and man in his royal grave pale, his blood shed.

Comment

Smell of sweat in the armpits dismays more
than the distant smell of the dead in a jungle war.
Possible and important are the blind date and alley but not
the blind man and his plight.

Heaven is curls in place
guipure over fine embroidered lace, leather
simulated, not mind membrane, human
skin woven together on an unknown face.

A clanger dropped at afternoon tea
is more shocking than a plane-load of bombs on Hanoi.
The canceling of a rugby match through rain
is more lamented than the canceling of a thousand men.

So let us cheer for our strange worldly wisdom in knowing
how to pack into our life's thrilling journey
such little happinesses that keep us determinedly going
to hell and back!

A Visit to the Retired English Professor

There in the grovertangle where sun-coltering stilth
galed down, splurned, merged into riper than cleamhold
warmermaze when its skin streakles pomperwelling in summer,
we flindered, melled, wimwalling, hintered.
                                                  Clone,
plene in his rale after so calid a time had milled its fee,
durant, he burndered, cleamed in the day's coltering zone.

Then we sat under the plum tree
on the wet grass-covered stone
while he talked of Hamlet.

The Family Doom

This gene is bred, cradled like my own son,
Heredity said when I demanded to know how
the family doom stays unchanging in its dugout
safe and snug while storms of sporting winds blow.

My time is too old, Heredity said,
to care for the half-million other traits
like happiness, that drift like thistledown in every sporting wind
while Doom, faithful homebody, stays.

Around the Rugged Rocks the Ragged Rascal Ran

This phosphorescent plate
with rugged edges
that are rocks not entwined roses

might heaving turn to serve up
a tongue twister from a drowned man's mouth
—a ragged rascal.

I remember him running and running along the beach
the cuts on his feet bleeding, his eyes staring wild.
And then he was floating in the sea, dead.
A ragged rascal, the people said.
They made us say it too, slowly and quickly to improve our speech.

Around the rugged rocks the ragged rascal ran.

I wonder did he know or care
that his suffering on that lonely South Island beach
might improve our speech?
Or did he understand and deplore
the too many trivial uses of adversity?

Wet Morning

Though earthworms are so cunningly contrived
without an opposing north and south wind
to blow the bones of Yes apart from the flesh of No,
yet in speech they are dumbly overturning,
in morning flood they are always drowned.

This morning they are trapped under the apple tree
by rain as wet as washing-day is wet and dry.
An abject way for the resilient anchorage of trees,
the official précis of woman and man,
the mobile pillarbox of history, to die!

Once

Once the warm draught of people
flowing under the locked door that held me from them
changed my flame, played
influence on my shadow,
burned re-burned me where I made
my tablets of wax in the dark.

Then beyond the door all was still.
Thief blackbird stopped up the keyhole
where birdbeaks of light, comforting, had pecked crumbs through.
A winter I could never know
sealed the cracks with an evil they called snow.
It was so pure, falling
from nowhere, its flakes blinding.

Beyond the door all was still.
I leaned in my lonely ritual.

Resolution

I'll not make a string of words
like cheap poppet-beads
to form my sentence of death
the circle that stops my breath.

The Sun Speaks at Perihelion

On the twelve Christmas days
I thought my gift and your treasure
would be my shining closest to earth.
Why did spires gouge out my eyes?
Why did the television crucifix
mingle my blood
with dancing girls, the Truth Game,
and the crisscross Quiz of Christ?

Atom

Now the blossom is sucked clean.
The bees policed in iron hives
control confuse threaten
the uncombed sweetness with power
to take lives by flash and fire.

It was an invisible flower
the nectar of worm and birth
an idea come up for air.
Iron bees, is it for new bread
or death the sweetness is spread?

Haworth Parsonage, Mt. Maunganui

(for E.P.D.)

This house: five headstones—five or any number
of senses, of dead, of fingers of the left hand
or lost world not sharing the secret,
climb, strapped with sand, salt-fed, bloom
white, alive, upon a morning trellis of cloud,

make summer houses where the living
command the sun behind tall glass,
to warm, not set fire to their tombs' autumn covering;
for leaves burn, mirrors break, Gerda-grime here
as in treeless Yorkshire may enflame their eyes.

Though never the five dead, coughing in fog
will feed this earth, yet, white stone your parsonage,
the house with its guavas, a lemon tree, hedge plants
wrapped in paper shawls against the frost; dank weed, castaway
            log,
sea-drowned wapiti antler the flower's full provision.

I Knew a Man

I knew a man one long time
whose heart had no real home;
I recall that he walked with a spirit-level
ceaselessly uphill, downhill.

He carved for his heart a flat tomb
in the tussock, and for many years kept warm
as a new-killed rabbit, till
he died at length of the sun's chill.

My Home

O the cold unpeeled hood
of my mushroom home
where sheep lie at night
on the warm oven-shelf of hillside
facing away from the south and the south wind
that on March days will drive
a comfortless other flock of thistledown,
turned out of house and home
given the white sack
with winter for last wage,
from summertime!

Pukeko

Pukeko, swamp hen
unescorted
is wearing junior navy
a pillarbox beak
burnt orange casual claws.

If shadow violates
will spear the dark
the damp lonely dark swamp
with hatpin scream
—Cree Cree!

The Peach

What has taken the peach in hand
to make it ripe so fur so
cover it so with gold mildew
like new decay spelling birth?

What time began it, what day
rolled it backward from sour stone
gathering thick moss of sun
on pathways thickest with worm?

When the Sun Shines More Years Than Fear

When the sun shines more years than fear
when birds fly more miles than anger
when sky holds more bird
sails more cloud
shines more sun
than the palm of love carries hate,
even then shall I in this weary
seventy-year banquet say, Sunwaiter,
Birdwaiter, Skywaiter,
I have no hunger,
remove my plate.

Chimney Fire

The shaking sou'west breath that will make
the telegraph wires moan and tell all their consuming
burden of messages in snow-clean confessional,
has panicked fire out of this heart and house, has raged
a passage of blood through soot
that may have choked or helped, like the black dust
that settles or battles with each coal of thought.

Summer

At midday then the sweltering mother
bedded in wheat and wharves rose
to give food
gold sea and salt bread to the city.

Deep from her blue apron pocket
she drew a ripe orange to slice
and squirt light
—your mouth was stained with sun.

Some Will Be for Burning

Some will be for burning, not all.
In the deep sky trees may lean, and men,
to take their hot gold coin, and some,
not all, will be for burning.

In autumn many trees have ashes for leaves;
the willow and the silver poplar
have paid the penalty of fire
no creek or soft rain will smother;

and there are men whose footfall on earth
is like the smoke and whisper of leaves.

But some will be for staying cold and whole
like stone in growth of moss, the green ember
kindled by creek water and soft rain.

Thought

Parsons and racegoers
bleed to death pondering.
The sea, till millennium's thirst,
walks up and down the platform
impatient for the tide.

Soon

Soon plucked and picked the bird
of world all gooseflesh to face winter
will plunge alone on wave of sky, furiously
trying to remember the furred moment
of leaf and feather.

New Year

The midnight moment—we have no wolves to howl
the moon but the drab morepork crying
with economical greed half its cry,
"Pork Pork Pork!"

This last night of December
the swollen moon-yolk approaches nearer
the earth, may drop a bright younker
fuming with feather,
or, infertile,
may waste or break or spill over
frying itself across the hotplate of January sky.

Tadpole

By frog I have escaped the indrawn teeth of black eel,
the long room of duck's mouth. Were I a man
should I not dance, leap, sing, prepare a five-year plan
or twenty-year or thirty till the sun burn through my soul?

But I, being soon frog only, how shall I explain
myself to myself, or tell of the dead year,
the escape from death in dark birth-circle of water,
the blackout into croaking light of my only plan?

Prejudice

Somebody has been in the bath too long,
somebody must soon pull out the plug,
drain away the dirty seas,
scour the tidemarks from the coast,
and with a secret ingredient (like truth)
dissolve the flotsam of old drowned bones
that were used as toys to distract, escape
from bathwater oceans of ideas that have got too dirty and
                too deep.

Her Thoughts

Her thoughts like poppies go to sleep in their clothes
with no west wind to iron out the creases in the morning.

The Sun

1

Now the sun
dark red
ladled across a bleak distance
shines warm
as evening cocoa
in an old man's home.

2

The sun
is a universal
shining
bank messenger
with a consuming inner life
and an Honors Degree in Perspective.

Dialogue

"People are strange?"

"Yes. They gave the rat of fear a brilliantine hairdress,
smoothed its bristle, preened its whiskers.
Clean and harmless as an ultra-bomb or refined plague
it followed like a poodle at the heels of their God.

"For exercise it walked upon the faith-lit Common
Ground of superstition; for breeding purposes it used

the free steepled stud opposite the Town Hall, the reserved
shelves of libraries, and cinemas showing expurgated films.

"How it earned the approval of their domestic hearts!
But—secret in the night, as the Rat of Fear, it gnawed
the stale furred slices of love, the half-tasted meal,
the torn letter of demand, refusal, transition
—all the overflowing garbage of their guilt."

"People are strange?"

"Yes, after the indifference of bees and lions
to small print, fossils, promises and disaster funds."

The Sanctuary of Hunger

In the Sanctuary of Hunger where the affluent seek
to escape the rotting of their plentiful fruit,
the sky snaps like a shell over the thrust-out hand
over the body collecting in futile pride
its free distribution of breath; head,
heart murmuring their ghostly depletions of tide.

An evil place, you say, which the affluent still need,
for in the Sanctuary of Hunger they know
the rumors of abundance of promised fruit
whose fables, like perennial visions ripening, never receive
the insinuating charity of decay.

Memory

Traffic and fashion have decreed
outmoded memories be thrown
in No Man's land where all men leave
the past machinery of their lives.

A mental bombsite, nothing more,
empty of peace, empty of war,
where too many mouths are locked
where too many hands fester
with wounds from broken wheels and rusting knives.

Words

"Words are for those with promises to keep."—W. H. Auden

On bicycle or foot following the fire engine to the fire,
smoke and fumes blowing into our eyes
from the paper mill the furniture and paint factory
the wooden house where two old brothers died swaddled in
        bedclothes.

Trained, uniformed, braided, words, powerful as ever,
rush in to the rescue, douse the dream cold.
We who are kept by promises have no hope of keeping them.
It is we who are given bed, board, a race after the siren,
permission to watch if we can get there before it's all over
while common nouns and verbs of doubtful origin control or
        kill the fire.

These Poets

These poets command the familiar working of
their merry-go-round of words and postures known.

Their pony or wild tiger syllables hop
terribly up and down in usual tune.

Mat quick Caesarian insight bring them word-cub
whimpering; toppling foal of poem one moment born.

Snow

A crime so frequent, so huge
of fraud and camouflage
would make it seem almost natural
the hurt world lying forever
                          locked in plaster
with some remembering the green
                                    underneath,
others never forgetting the
                          fracture.

Furniture

Idiots are not all a smile and a wide plain
with the sun concentric in their eyes;
but a straw room, food to sleep with,
a stairway to straddle, and all belonging
put back to their secret mouth.

They do not talk wisely like wise men,
though wise men
seeing the uncluttered room of an idiot
may envy him his wisdom in not knowing three things—
how to compare,
how much furniture should have been there,
and where it has gone.

The Sunflowers

You said the sunflowers when they bloomed
would from morning till night face the sun,
turning each hour their huge heads cushioned with fire
pinned with black seed.
It was an old old story you believed in.

Later, before Christmas, when your flowers unfolded
they turned brilliant cold shoulder to the sun's ember,
they faced south. Does the sun,
after all, shine from there? Could it be proved?
Tell me, what did you think, you
who believed in this old old story?
Did you twist the stems of your flowers, extinguishing
their cremative emblem, think, Bury the faithless,
not, Praise their self-consuming? Or still believing
in an old old story, gathering years of broom petals,
dropped gorse from dusty roads, grapefruit from the dark wintry
                    room,
did you build your own truth of new sun,
think, Praise the faithful for their choosing?

Cold Snap

It was the timed wave the toffee-wave
breaking where the cold-water cup
was a cliff of clean tooth
tasting the syrup of decay.

It is the secret frost feeding the night
the ripe as winter sweet set
like ice (when cold cut in squares)
of havoc for the summer's tooth.

Hotel, Cambridge

On the eighth floor every morning I met
a pale middle-aged man limping with a stick
along the corridor. I traveled in the lift with him.
He did not speak.
He's a distinguished scholar, I thought.
He's come here to die within sight of Havard Square,
his old University, the dogwood and maple leaves and the gray
        squirrels.
Warm in this luxury hotel he'll die as he lived,
his chair drawn close to the chosen fire.

And after death, knowing he is a man of sin
who without repentance
could turn a comma from its comfortable sentence,
could in cold language strangle a newborn thought,
some other faculty of truth
exorbitantly charging host
will decide his fate.

People Are Ill, Dying

People arc ill, dying. The skin
like that of a mushroom
is peeled from the flesh. The body
is not poisonous after all.

It sprang up overnight
under the sky in the dew
where a warm sheep
snuggled asleep
and in its center stalk
a worm lay.

Mysterious night origins
rain of centuries of hate
dung and dew
the worm in the pillar
the ceiling of flesh
the sun on the roof.

Is this proof
that man is an edible fungus,
a mere breakfast treat
to be fried by bomb's explosion,
eaten by nothingness of death?

Dunedin Walk

Today as I walk through the Botanical Gardens
I think of Nikita Khrushchev and the peasant sayings
   he might have found in Dunedin.

"It is better to keep a rogue elephant as ornament in your front
   window
than a live pine tree with its roots aching in your heart."

"With every sting a bee perishes. Death is more alkaline
than baking soda and its formula is always variable."

"Ducks on a muddy pond may not be numbered accurately.
   The curse
of arithmetic is that it thrives in stillness,
its true focus is seen only in death.
Do not be deceived by the pool's irrelevance.
Men as well as ducks are amphibious creatures."

"There was an old man, a Hillside Worker, who once glimpsed the
   Governor General.
Is he entitled to a smile and handshake fifty years later?

Representatives are not people
except when they touch. Then there is proof
they have skin that renews itself every seven years
and freckles and burns in the sun."

"It is not the agony of the poor dead or the dead poor
that they cannot butter their bread
only that they may not eat or talk or kiss.
It is the agony of the living
the dead should grieve like this
when winter is solely dependent on
the willingness of green leaves to die."

"A sound shell where a brass band plays
only on fine days and holidays
is like a sheep farmer
who goes to the wool sales
to sneer at the fleece of his own flock."

Mother and Son

My mother said to my brother, "Dearest child
that you may not choke and die
I will cut your meat into small pieces
I will remove the bones from the chicken and the fish
that you might eat without fear; that is my wish."

"Mother, mother, a strange meal approaches, too huge
with too many bones.
                        It is pushed before me
on a plate as wide and round as the sky,
on a table of grass and forest.
                        Our cupboard never held
a knife to slice it nor had you hands to tear
the flesh apart from so many bones growing thick as trees.
O mother, mother, I will choke and die!"

47

My mother said to my brother, "Dearest child,
is your meal so strange and fearful?
                                        It is I."

The Kea Speaks from the Dunedin Botanical Gardens

I have learned to walk upside down like a fly
while my neighbor three cages away cries, Woe O Woe.
I can sense, though not see, the sky.

I too, like you, have a ceiling of wire to my aspirations,
while the peach-faced lovebirds huddle together close to the earth
and the wekas move like small brown brooms through the rushes.

If you were to write a poem about me you would say, Pity
the kea's imprisonment. But it would be yourself you pitied
in your own prison, for though you can both sense and see the sky
you have not yet learned to walk upside down like a fly.

Dunedin Story

I brought a leper into my house.
I gave him the spare room with the panel-end bed, the flock
                    mattress, the spare blankets and sheets
and the duchesse with the oval mirror
that, swinging back and forth, reflects a person from head to foot.

"I have traveled a long way," my leper said.
"I had to wait many years before they gave me a permit to come
                    here.
I had to be investigated, examined,
sponsored,

and then at last
I was accepted.
I shall get treatment here
from the hospital on Cumberland Street.
I shall sleep in your spare room, have meals with you,
walk down through the Botanical Gardens under the Ponderosa
Pine trees
across the bridge
past the Otago Savings Bank Centennial Kiosk
past the pensioners' houses on Duke Street.
And then one day when I am cured I will go to the Labor
Exchange and find a job.
How happy I am to be accepted into your country!"

The neighbor clipping his hedge looked over at me.
"I hear you've a leper staying with you," he said. "Isn't it
dangerous?"
I answered with the best argument.
"Oh they wouldn't have admitted my leper if they thought that,"
I said.
"You know they're very careful about that sort of thing."
"I suppose you must be right," my neighbor said. "All the same
I'd watch out if I were you."

The woman tending the deep-freeze in the grocer's lifted the
steak and egg sausage carefully out of its
bed beside the chicken and onion sausage.
"I hear you've a visitor," she said. "Is he staying long?"
"Oh he's making his home here."
"He's from overseas?"
"Yes. My leper. He's come to be cured."
The woman frowned. "Yes, I've heard that," she said.
And after I began to walk from the shop I noticed she rubbed her
hands on a small towel hanging on a rail behind the door.

The front of my house reeked of disinfectant.
Men from the Council

had arrived and were cleaning the footpath.
"The city's taking no chances," the foreman said.

Months passed. Spring came, and summer, and autumn,
                and winter
when the rain stayed clogged in the long grass and the dead
leaves flapped against the twigs
and fog, mingled with smoke, settled like snow in the valleys.
My leper was stricken with a strange disease
that none could diagnose.
It was, they said, a disease
worse than leprosy, worse than any other,
hardest to be cured of,
a fatal disease where the sufferer may yet last a lifetime
in agony and mutilation.

They said he had caught the disease from the neighbors cutting the
                the hedges,
from the woman serving in the deep-freeze counter in the grocer's,
from the Council men spraying disinfectant outside my front door,
and—worst blow of all—they said he had caught it from me,
from my use of the possessive pronoun.
"Did you not talk of him," they reminded me, "as *your* leper?
My leper, you said. *My* leper this and that.
The disease of being at once outlawed and owned is worse than
                leprosy.
It is, simply, terribly,
the indestructible virus
the gift of the living who are blind
to the living who are believed dead."

The Treadmill

O madness the blinkered horse trod
with such delicacy upon the treadmill
bringing up pure water from the well
from blanketing shadow of early morning
through noon to night; crops are fed,
grow, fruit, ripen, are harvested,
eaten, excreted as dust-white dust
under the hooves of the blinkered horse.

I remember the sun, I remember the sun,
length breadth acreage, the square
miles of fields bordered with olive trees.
I remember the sun, I remember the sun
whose circle is my smallest world
fire earth and pure water from the deepest well,
and man, blind man, and his goad
with the chief indefinite article removed to make God.

Dream

Tiny people in a tiny tilled field
(which God can hear the grass grow?)
my teeth in black cases were black
like coffins; I had eaten
dates that stuck to my teeth; I had
eaten time and hastened my own decay.
Which God can hear the grass grow
and the wool on a sheep's back?

Cat Spring

At this time of year strangers lurk in my garden.
Their cry gobbles the snow-encircled full moon,
their alley-hunger makes a sexual slum
of a city that is rumored to be clean. I
                              never trust
                                       rumor.
Beware, Dunedin!
                    The cats are out of the bag at last.
                                        The chambers
of night commerce are full to overflowing.
It is spring.
          The gardens hold immeasurable loot of gold
crocuses, silk-
              veined daffodils
                        stained lust of
                                    tomcats'
                                          milk.

Sparrows Climb the Stair

Sparrows climb the stair,
smoke makes an archway,
the holiday children steer
gocarts in the street of yellow hedges;
and the little ring-eyes never fly alone.

Paths of snow on the hills
higher than we remember or know
above the town of slowest growth
where mayor and councilors cry
for industry
and feasting on suet and honey
the little ring-eyes never fly alone.

52

Born in a Gentle Country

Born in a gentle country
mothered by peace and mercy
I've never learned to stay in the forbidding House of Judgment
where guests are warned to speak one sentence only,
"Humanity is no excuse for Humanity."

I've discovered it's not mercy
nor peace nor being born in a gentle country
that deters me: the rent is too high
decision on decision paid out to a total
terrifying lifelong responsibility.

Besides, who is to know whether the true owner, Love,
who first toiled and planted the walled garden, may wander now,
himself an insane prisoner in the House of Judgment?

Beginnings

Up the crocuses,
and they are struck down;
up the crocuses again
old-gold, and they dare not open.

I'll not see them this year,
their first year in a new bed,
tangled in the cold sheets of the earth
enforced guests of the sleeping sun

that refuses to wake into light and prepare breakfast.
O struck down
broken at the stem
their magnificent heads wound in a golden scarf.

Up the crocuses
to try a third time
one morning to feed
their innocent faces with light?

53

Early Spring

Nothing doing
except at the foot of the stem
closest to earth
a rub of green leaf

almost in bloom;
a winter-lost bud
found, clothed again by the storm
of memory's green dust.

The Reply

Yes, I remember that afternoon in winter, how
before we climbed the hill to the cattle shed
we thought to look for shelter in an empty house
but were told, No Admittance. Trespassers
Will Be Prosecuted. Keep Out.
                                    . Strangely,
it was John, the youngest who alone accepting the words' meaning
reminded us that the hammering of the human will upon words
may not always change them, though poets,
I'm sure you've said and others have said, are blacksmiths
who sweat at the forge to bend and twist the shape
and patterns of language. (My two grandfathers
were blacksmiths. They made fire-tools, shovels, tongs
to feed and control the fires; and horseshoes
trampled by nightmares fragmenting the stars with their fury.)

So we came to the cattle shed, and it was
as you have described it, and I spoke of Andorra,
though here there were no mountain dogs, no white
and blue violets with their scent stolen by the snow,
nor hot springs nor small square of land growing tobacco
and tobacco strung to dry, nor cattle with winter-black gaze
flank to flank in the straw- and dung-smelling dark.
Also, we'd had no bowls of bread and milk for breakfast.

I remember our joy at being in the place. There was nowhere
to sit or stand. The cattle before us
had made no provision for our comfort, not
aware perhaps that our thinking bulk
churns with ideas and feelings and transformations
other than flesh into beef and grass into milk.
                                        Or are we
so different?
              Yes, Jacquie and I squatted on the floor; we made
the living hieroglyph that John will tell you about
if you don't already know: the gesture that portrays birth,
for the memories of women and cattle sheds are enduring;
how the strangers were given warning, No Admittance.
                    Keep Out. No Vacancy.

Yes, I remember that afternoon in winter,
but I remember chiefly how the cold and wet became
more cold and wet than we could bear, and like exiles
we talked of home, of how to get there,
of how in the evening we'd sit around the manuka fire;
you hurried on ahead to make the dream come true.

You may remember that it didn't happen that way. Reality
took command.
              You,
Jacquie and John went home. I went home. Later,
disguised, wearing a cannibal starfish as ornament, I saw
you both, disguised also, among the academic pastures

(Trespassers Are Not Prosecuted. Welcome. Vacancy.)
eating savories, cud-chewing with the visiting professor
who had been led, lowing gently, to be milked
of expert opinions of the N.Z. cultural scene.

Poets

Poets are not afraid to drown.
The dry people of the dry world walk on
wanting to dive in yet not having learned
to swim or administer mouth-to-mouth breathing.
The poet is a poor fish, they say. Leave him.
O Tom Dick and Harry
Mabel Mildred and Cora,
What is that tide flowing out of the room and into the street?
Somebody's best-kept words have got out.
We are in danger of wet feet!

O Tom Dick and Harry
Mabel Mildred and Cora
from foot to ankle to thigh
(Oh! hot on the scent of me, a rude noun!)
higher and higher the tide is flowing.

And we are not fish rich nor poor
and we can neither swim nor drown.

Wyndham

The big stick
has given up stirring
the Wyndham pool.

56

Stones do not move here;
people sleep while
the cows make milk
the sheep make wool

and in the empty
railway houses
no Dad sits each morning
on the satin-smooth
dunny seat.

Curiosity, Custom, Hunger, Fear, and Sound

It makes one curious
curiosity
—how strange these strange things may be!
The whole weight of their being, once named,
topples like a mountain stone into the mind
to stay planted
taken for granted
at home.

It makes one accustomed
—custom.

It makes one hungry
—hunger
as iron makes the ironmonger.

It makes one fearful
—fear
as sound discovers its being reason in
the ear.

Duties

To buy a shank of mutton
for an old widow-woman
who lies in bed sick
with an aching back.

To cook the shank of mutton
with a carrot and an onion
a turnip and potato
while the fire burns low.

To serve a bowl of soup
to do the washing-up
to smooth the ruffled bed
and the pillow at her head.

To fill the coal scuttle
put out the milk bottle
hook that latch tight
of the creaking gate.

Then look in on Monday
Tuesday Thursday and on **Sunday**
on Wednesday and on **Friday**
to keep her house tidy

then to gaze at her slyly
and not wonder why
with her life run dry
she fails to die.

Flo

Flo's dead.
Go down, God.
Magnificent with curses
with judgment
the Moving Finger points
and having pointed
not all your delicate death announcements in the newspaper
your hiding of the fact
that she died you know where
in a back ward mad
can alter her white-haired splendor as I knew her
spokeswoman for God (who else ever dared?)
commanding with her mountain frown
the cruellest world ever made to Go Down, Go Down
the dark Well
of Hell
and Drown.

Dream

In the jungle again, named as little monkeys
swinging from branch to branch, on the jungle floor climbing
over dead logs fallen in the night from the mightiest tall trees,
going somewhere, three of us, escaping. A glance over the shoulder
discovers the pursuing leopard with long spotted fur and the head
                and open mouth of a python,
the once friendly fabulous beast that walked quietly on a leash
led by the old wise inhabitant of the jungle,
now raging out of control, its mouth open wide to swallow us.

Us, I say? But I think only of myself. It must not capture me.
Gida! I cry. Help, Gida!
The last tree on the jungle floor becomes a cliff. I struggle to
                climb over it. My monkey's paws become human
                hands

not able to grasp the fibers of the dead tree
that are torn away like uprooted plants in my hands. I cry again
>for help,
Gida, Gida!

Then I read before me in the illuminated manuscript,
Of the three, none escaped.

Gida is the past participle of God.

For Zarene Rose

Named on your first day—was this wrong
or too sudden after waking?

Dressed as your name; lying also
at the edge of letters, looking down
where silence does not seem strange.

Knowing a small adequate hunger; calm taking.

Your mother writes to me:
Zarene Rose is now five days old.
She cries little and sucks well.
Her fingers are long, like mine.

Or like the fingers of the elmbuds in spring?

This Is the Forest

"This is the forest primeval, the murmuring pines and the
>hemlock."

These are part of my life's takings
from the till of word-mystery.
Cream salt seeds of hemlock syllables

drop in my hair and lap
and in my body's and mind's eye.

Congregations lean their heads to pray
for brown cloth books of needle words
to mend the earth, for God-sway haloed
with blue sky. Let me out:
the darkness is a cry of birds.

Merchant of Mammon and Prayer I sold
the long lasting aniseed sun
and bought a new disconsolate world
of wordless murmuring
wailing where nothing new is known,

where drawn beneath the rust-stained blanket
the perfect sentence of sleep lies
wrapped in dark word-earth of forests.
Ripe cones bursting feed bright
speech-rockets to the silent fires.

The Chrysalids

As a child not more sensitive than others
I used to pick the gray-walled chrysalids
for fishing bait, and afterwards feast well
on the rainbow and brown trout my father caught.
Now, exiled from the crawling flying creatures
that once mistook my hair for red shrubbery,
barley grass, a mossy forest, I feel compassion
for the world I robbed. I remember those windowless
gray houses of sober unusual design;
hanging dungeons dependent on the frail
life-security of attachment to leaves;
houses with walls gray-folded, pleated
like the robes of monks; frayed hairshirts,

old sackcloth sealed at top and tail; dull
colonies and clusters that never showed light;
deep shelters with the occupants, asleep,
unable to receive or comprehend
the wildfire rumor spreading from red leaf
to red leaf that the world was nearing its end,
that a new world, in seclusion, was being made complete.

I did not know. I would never have believed
that every house I stole contained a jewel.
I gathered them as if they had been overripe fruit,
I thought their mud-colored walls withered
and ugly and useful only for fishing bait.
And now I feel compassion. Is it too late
to soften to a new shape and dimension the hard truth
that parallel worlds must never meet?

The Pocket Mirror

So many thousand times a minute
the light from the street lamps goes out.

I have devised a method by which this may be shown
to those to whom the facts of light are unknown.

Taking this pocket mirror, capture the reflection
of the row of lamps. Steady the mirror. So.

See those black stripes alternating with yellow?
They are bars of actual darkness not perceived by the naked eye.

To undeceive the sight a detached instrument like a mirror is
          necessary.
The human senses never speak the truth if they can get away with
          an easy lie.

Tigers on the prowl? Tar spread with butter?

Master Dark
in his sergeant's coat?

A black cat on a bed of cheese?
Goldfinch feathers? Clay and cypresses? A sandwich of Heaven
            and Hell?
Caterpillars looping the length of street
feeding on darkness to become morning butterflies?

What can I say but that you are burdened with lies.
You babble of sun pollen, honey plight
of black tulips; you repeat that you *know*
when you are clearly ignorant of the facts of light
and intend to remain so.

Wait! Give me back my pocket mirror. Were it to break
I should have no clear sight, and seven years' bad luck!

At Night

At night across my window I see
the shadow of a stair and a tossing tree.
I know they are really there, outside,
but I am afraid.

The moon shining down
splinters the roofs of the town;
the street lights in glory
that is awkward and without reward
and does not make plants and people grow,
stand alone revealing the emptiness
varnishing the gray streets with unrequited light
that is a desert festival,
a banquet that no one wants to eat.

Lying half-asleep I am spring cleaning
the lived-in quarters of my dreaming.

63

I throw away the horror and fear
(I think) beyond the window, but they stay,
they stay there in the shadow on the blind
of the nameless tossing tree and the dark stair.

O the harm of harmlessness
the leaking guilt that makes a morass
of innocence until at last
sleep, like swamp lilies, blossoms there!

Country Dead

Except in times of epidemic and war
the sight of human remains is rare.
White-skulled cattle with splintered horns
hips of sheep, huge horseflanks like shovels,
chicken wishbones
—these provide the image of human friend, family and stranger
                who die
—I mean, in our country.

In childhood they said, Take Uncle Henry's dead hand.
I never held it as I held closely
the rabbit's paw until the fur had rubbed off,
though Uncle Henry also lay caught in a shining oblong trap
and was thrust out of sight in the cold earth
and the world's weather never had a chance
to set Uncle Henry or anyone I knew, polished and clean
in tussock, matagouri, snow grass,
as properly finished dead people of bone.
It was only surmise that made their image, in the dark,
resemble the lost animals I had known
who surely lounged upstairs sun-bathing their gray skulls and
                growing
grass hair in a permanent golden wave and wearing
white mushroom sun hats each morning new.

O the brazen extravagance of the country dead!
Aunties May, Lily, Marigold and Uncle Henry.
Aunties May, Lily, Marigold, and Uncle Henry!

Beach

Here is an empty bulb of transparent jelly
whose light swam within; we regret
our houses are not such even with ceiling to floor
glass windows nor are we our own illumination,
yet we stay, we do not abandon house
to return to the sea that abandoned us
as flick-knife brain unfolding to cut through cell walls
and form some attachment to growing.
                                        Sea grapes
cluster white on the white sand. Wave on wave tills the old
                vineyard; kelp
carcasses, amber and green armor still worn shifting
the dead thing from upper to lower wave in expectation of
battle of tide grenades foam-bursting blossoming
to crush what tries to grow or having died to move even after death,
to join the commotion of going that waves are, eternally.
Eternally?
            Caution putting a sheltering hand over this word
to stop it like a candle flame from going out
(though who uses candles now?) commands, Don't. Let the word
            be, in its corner of the world
burning for ever, being what it is, without energy for sentences.

                    Some seaweed
cast out of the sea though not outcast
is like lace woven into leaf patterns; some is like a forest
of dead bulls with horns still waving.
We walk on the sand. We do not make three-toed footprints.

How proud we are, then, of our five toes!
Dogs run, bark at the sea, leave their forked prints; gulls fold,
unfold, their paper wings poised
beyond the green glazed window.

School is not out. Four-square country school, the iron-skirted
bell swinging aloft, the dental clinic smell,
the playground caved and pitted as if asphalt in geological guise
tries against time to record time
beside the venerable sea rocks skipped on, played on
by generations of waves dancing, stamping impatient triumphant
        sun-filled idleness.

A woman hastens with late afternoon shopping, otherwise
the street beside the sea is deserted. The curtains are drawn
in the white holiday houses.
In the gardens young plants battered beyond their years lean
on manuka sticks and taste their tears returned by the wind and
        the spray.
                    The tide is almost in.
No rockpools. No shells. Only the thunderous display
of waves deceptively smooth suddenly on nearing the shore
giving up the tremendous ghost of their blossom
over and over and over, dragging a groan heavy, entangled as
        seaweed
from the throat of the watcher.
                    The groan
is the only language that without thought
will encompass the meaning.

Thinking will, in time, unravel the ancient knot of despair.
                    Words
will drop like pearls from the sheltering loops.
It is writers rather than boyscouts who must investigate the
        culture of knots, learn
to pitch words by the sea, to make
fire with less than two vowels rubbed together
and name it other than the groan of despair.

Jungle Fruit

A snake is hissing in the undergrowth
but I am safe: I have eaten the jungle fruit.
Snakes are patterned like linoleum
but without flowers, and polished
by the absent sun into diamonds and circles
that startle with danger; but I am safe,
I have eaten the jungle fruit.

The first time it was bitter and I spat it out.
The second time the taste of it made tears come to my eyes.
The third time I tried to swallow it whole and then
it stuck in my throat,
and I was dumb for seven years and a day and night.

I am speaking now in the sunlight and firelight,
in the green world while the snake's head
golden and flat as a penny
lies unspent among the stones.

Dying

Dying, the accountant who skated
on thin ice was rated
an Obituary in the morning paper
(the *Otago Daily Times*)
that made no mention of crimes,
called him neither embezzler nor raper
but told of his various memberships sailing
to charitable waters
and how he left a young widow wailing
and one son and two daughters.

In a career of managing pounds and pence
he should have accumulated enough sense
(forty is a mature age)
to heed the warning advice:
Beware. No skating. Dangerously thin ice.

Or was his death simply a final marriage
of principle and practice?

The Spell

Into one medium-sized sliced-pineapple tin
left overnight to gather Northeast Valley household
smoke, and fog surrounding the green farm on the valley
slope where each morning sheep bleat and dogs bark,
                                        put one thread
of crocus budded two days, one frost petal from a south-facing
windowpane, one flame from a garden bonfire,
one beam from a peak-hour television program,
enough light to flood, darkness to fill
the four leaks in the kitchen roof that will never be mended.

Then taking as much as a skyful of Swampy Clouds,
a haul that everyone will say is impossible,
geranium-red clouds, tussock-brown, silver and pearl, sea gull
                color,
bomb-shape, blossom-shape, stir
and over the brew keep watch all night with rain
until the spell erupting into vivid morning
miraculously overflows the pink and white terraces of sky,
and light on inspection, descends,
gentle with early daffodils but flashing crude
mirrors to date more precisely the wrinkled
local specimens of human skin.

The time drops into history and the history books.
Questions are asked—
What was the picture of life before the Spell?
Within dying memory was it all so cruel?
No one wants to remember.
The green and gold lava of spring has set,
                              completing
                                    the burial.

A Golden Cat

As I walked to my office one day and stopped
by the flax bushes near the curve of the road
to look at the view of the city and Northeast Valley
and the amber poplars with the light shining through them,
and all the autumn trees turning where turn still means decay,
the souring of the once freshly foaming season,

a golden cat came out of the bushes, wove
around my feet, said, Own Me, Own me, I am golden.
Scorched flax, leaves, berries on fire, none
come so gracefully to you; it is I
who am the weaving golden season.

I hurried on thinking perhaps I dreamed it.

Mother and Daughter

Gay strawberry tassels hang from the arbutus.
Irresistibly persuaded, raindrops separate
from clinging leaves. Water easily will let go
its trembling hold when earth force reaches up to tug it free.

Half-green, half-yellow, the sycamores are shabby with waiting.
Their windmill seeds, knowing

the routine, travel blindfold past withered
stalks that languidly admit, It can happen here.

Custom lies heavier than death upon the scene.
The watching eye must look away to discover
Proserpine ugly, unpredictably human,
abhorring white lilies, roses, saffron flowers,

while her mother, blond Ceres, does not care so late
to tramp cornfield and street to discover where,
in what underground hovel, with whom
her wayward daughter sleeps six months of the year.

Yet concern and love are told still in the moss-burning strawberries
and the young raindrops, without will, sliding into the earth,
and the wind, awake all night, helping in the search for what is
        lost,
and the glistening white face of the frost against the morning
        window.

Lament for the Lakes

The colback talkus
the lacklegion worcle
the dindle pyrrage
all in fusive query have tanquished
the plion's domacious thrave.

Barevolved craffhanded turbuked
under driftices of berge
damperly they have sultured
mormed without crumbience or zone
each tressled pave.

How often the clamber has griped
murplained in full bondary and plexment

against roamage, thorm strild
vout sordure disencloming the dupely lakened seethe!

Circumless dranion has cunneived
has tranced it without requining
where only the pribed sparrion
crope turbly crysically
the rigilant endeethe

and angletamed with armile
the dislatched wolmew clangs
heedily this downage ominime
in foil and bondary, murplains from grope
to grope its alpave

where at furmess, dragly com, wim
with magerman strifle
still the colback talkus the lacklegion worcle
the dindle pyrrage
brackly tanquish the plion's thrave.

The Cabbages

The leaves that sheltered the cabbage heart became
coarse, thick veined with the labor of growing.
They lay flat, covered with dust, invisibly seamed
to the tough low-squatting stem that, knuckled and notched,
still lived to remind the blind root that after
the tender heart has been cut out cabbages still grow.

Fate is a consuming snowfall of white butterflies, a cow's
hoof crushing, torn leaves thrust through the wire netting into
          the fowl run
to be pecked at, eaten.
          Winter.
              All the cabbages have gone

save a few battered leaves. Each plant that gave without protest
its newly-formed heart, its core of being, its growing reason,
receives the blessing of emptiness and age:
Frost on a gray head
a long thirst satisfied
by glinting dewfall
returned again and again
to the sun, as treasure.

The Suicides

It is hard for us to enter
the kind of despair they must have known
and because it is hard we must get in by breaking
the lock if necessary for we have not the key,
though for them there was no lock and the surrounding walls
were supple, receiving as waves, and they drowned
though not lovingly; it is we only
who must enter in this way.

Temptations will beset us, once we are in.
We may want to catalogue what they have stolen.
We may feel suspicion; we may even criticize the décor
of their suicidal despair, may perhaps feel
it was incongruously comfortable.

Knowing the temptations then
let us go in
deep to their despair and their skin and know
they died because words they had spoken
returned always homeless to them.

The City

Light alone is pledged to search forever
to rebuild the ancient city of winter
to force man beast bird and flower to remember,
and remembering relearn with alarm
cunning and skill the same spell
that an old man's skinny-armed embrace
dreams of each night between the kapok and the clay:
in the dark it is light not death that uncovers
the lost city and the living crocus.

On Reading a Book of Poems

A strange experience I had when reading your poems. I
held each page up to the light
to try to read, also, the shadow poem: a page is a narrow
place to hide or be stored in; yet these held fully-rooted
blossoming flowers, not blowaway flattened seed
changing posture at a breath. I might
have torn or cut the pages but that
would not have been wise. A poet's
labor of love must be matched in
his publisher (here the Oxford University Press)
by a love of labor.
(Otherwise the poet might offer his next work to Faber!)

So I was not destructive. I returned to the poems themselves.
You should have heard the jingling of keys
as the words announced a massive coming of age.
Each word held a key labeled,
Take One. Don't kid yourself they are free.
The User Pays.
What a magnificent party it must have been on that last night!
Then—sleep, wakening to responsibility, license to vote, kill,

and a huge repair bill from hope—paid chiefly
by God and the sea, innocent of age,
and poems, poems riding day and night through the storm,
coming safe to harbor.

I took a key.
I entered the hold between the pages and the lines where the
              poems lay.
I had no lavender-perfumed
                        insecticidal spray
for fear a carpenter ant might get into the country
and erode the foundations of respectability
or a stink strike
from the foul human heap (in poetic monarchy
the joker is always dealt on top of the poor Queen)
nor was I afraid of beetles flying direct from the sun,
stowaways within the poem.

How does it feel to own so many ships?
But of course you are right,
you, rich owner, to register your fleet
under the white foam-flag of death:
in that way you gain entry to all countries,
trading in a rare language that at first we taste, spit out, then
              long for.
It's a tough life,
but you are safe enough
nursed on the wide blue breast of ocean.

Our Town

The raging and the ravenous
the tiger in the tiger-pit.
"Shall I write pretty poetry?"

Bewildered in the morning down dry roads
I came, hungry and yet not starved.

I encountered the crowd returning from amusements:
I saw old duchesses with their young lovers.
(But for lust we could be friends;
leave Helen to her lover. Draw away.
Now I can see what Helen was.)

In our town people live in rows
—the raging and the ravenous
the tiger in the tiger-pit.
"Shall I write *pretty* poetry?"

I have with fishing rod and line
caught a cosmic Leviathan, that monstrous fish.
Damn it all! This our south stinks peace!
. . . I idly cut a parsley stalk.

The Garden called Gesthemane,
the old professor of Zoology . . .
Mother Carey (she's the mother of the witches)
the curate and the spinster sit
in the first year of the last disgrace.
Hermes Trismegistus,
Sempronius.
Priapus with his God's virility.
Abelard was; God is
a householder in goathooves;
presume that in this marble stable
never
at Dirty Dick's and Sloppy Joe's
Christmas declares the glory of the flesh.

. . . Shall I make pretty poetry?
Downhill I came, hungry and yet not starved
to the Garden Gesthemane.
(Isn't the violet a dear little flower? And the daisy too?)
At Dirty Dick's and Sloppy Joe's
in our town people live in rows.

Overlooked

Three bungalows double-brick bay-windowed
retained by concrete walls and hedges
and their gardens' mainstay of geraniums
promising, after the feared avalanche, the brightest
bloodflow into drab Northeast Valley—

these squat in my eyes, on my head, are sacked
on my shoulders as fuel weight for the fires
I choose to light and be warmed by.
Waking, sleeping, their blinds go up and down.
The Fates never knew so polished an armory of shears
nor practiced so
upon the cursed people growing like hedges.

In my turn overlooking, I beat down
on roofs below the rejected words
that crop up overnight in my wild garden.
(I let my long grass grow undisturbed
to drink its morning dew, scatter seed, bead and light.)

Using my eyes and other weapons
I, in the mountain-looking order
attack the underlings in the valley who, crouching
in the mist, lean close to the earth
with craters and graves beneath them
while the dead under their scrutiny
turn uneasily
overlooking the center, fire burn.

Look up, look down. Somewhere, lovers know,
is the union of stone and cloud.
Though neighbors and their geraniums may be one
and the hedges they trim be as lovely as a kissed hem.
neighbor to neighbor does not flow as lovers do.
Their walls retain; and up and down and down
the blinds go, and the eyes,

and hedged by the lower dead, by returning words,
by geraniums and walls retaining
the blood and burial power of earth
today or tomorrow I too taking
my sharpened fate in my hand
below, above,
will destroy to survive.

Poem of Sight

Fore—
juts brow, shelf
intruding-most self,
skin closes
petals over roses,
cast arm, court and father
go and gather
hand gift, lock and head,
name shore and noon-mast peak.

Eye—
blinkful
lashful tooth-wink
witness-glass brow bath
sore shot and service.

In—
born and breathe,
deed firm
flame land and roadside;
patient, tend and set urn
complete.

The Flowering Cherry

These cherries are not wine-filled bowls for thirsty birds
nor ornaments of the house where sky's the ceiling.
These are the pawnbroker tree's discreet sign,
the wine, tear and blood drops of bondage,
the tree's relentless advantage
taken of the poverty that came when, warmed
with familiar memory of what had been
and had been and would be but is never known
entirely or believed until it is born,
we saw the cherry tree in flower, and at once spent
a life's rich astonishment.

"Why should I be bound to thee?"
Blake asked of the myrtle tree. Why?
He killed to escape. Blood flowed beneath the tree:
a father's blood, and old man's, who must have known
how to bargain with all possession
that makes a tree, a house, a sky into a prison
and each man see the marks of chains upon his skin.

The cherry tree flowers earlier than most,
falls as snow while snow is still falling
sweeps into us and through us and we taste
the flower as fruit, we eat the first
full-blown light unfolded out of winter darkness.
Then, as if the bloom were gone, the tree will hide
in wine-colored shade and pawn signs to pursue its trade.

And we are prisoners then, borrowing wonder
to redeem the pledge; or too poor, too ill,
too far away to make the necessary journey,
we plead in writing for the tree's mercy. Why
should a lifetime of marveling be spent
on this first view of spring light, this burst of cherry snow?
Why should the tree house, our treasure in blood?

When next you pass the flowering cherry now, in September,
look closely at the cool dark wine house
where the blackbirds sing for their supper
where the human senses sing for their survival.

Last Will and Testament

When collade wolders fail
when cabled I lie mead
then let this will be read,
my realty understood:

To Grapneline who loitered me
I leave my dimmer whurl.
To Grange, Able and Dully
my slate solstice pearl.

To Furner Done, my distant claim
I leave my sendal humorsome
seniority of burying
with its churnel osmend harrowing.

To Larceny who fetted wing
wole and durstimion, a cilice thing
I leave—my new larch
to quinquilt his bones in March.

So much I have, so much I leave
when collade wolders fail.
Thus let my will be read,
my realty understood.

The Farenheit Man

The farenheit man
on the centigrade sea
with wittage and wantage
and wastage and me

filling the billen
with ices and tea
for Cynewulf's baggard
boggard, higgard
wittage wantage
wastage and me

the farenheit man
is so cruel to me
I paddle alone
on the centigrade sea
for wittage wantage
Cynewulf's baggard
boggard, higgard
have gone from me
to tropical summer
to simmer and shimmer
to quimmer and quammer

wittage wantage
wastage, Cynewulf's baggard
boggard higgard
the farenheit man
are so cruel to me
alone on the centigrade sea.

My Mother Remembers Her Fellow Pupils at School

Dorcas Dyden
Hetty Peak and Ruby Blake.
Kate Rodley
Lucy Martella
Dorcas Dryden
Hetty Peak and Ruby Blake
Kate Rodley
Lucy Martella.

Dorcas Dryden . . .

The People

Against the grain the people go
into dark knots, polished,
identifiable, strong, the praised blemish.

Within the grain, thin, palely
their lives thread the difficult
dark-slanted eye of history.

Against against within within
more secret patterned historic than wood grains
flows the blood in people's veins.

Wars rage gales blow tides flow
against, within the grain the people go.

He Swam Like a Stone

He swam like a stone
the link was small
between his body
and the deep well.

Mud oozed from his eyes
a flowing thread
of green weed
parceled him dead.

Flesh and water
once knew how
to live together
at heart flow.

The Mountain

Yet the room seemed empty, the bed
honestly flat and white like a blank appointment card
(since through arranged meetings we try to control
our body's landscape) or a plain with any deceptive shadowy
hideout of trees and bushes burned by a long summer.

Therefore the hand mustered, commanded neatness, the future
                spread
thin and safe as oilskin;
the mind made its plan—

forgetting the restless traveling to and from appointments,
stations, conventions,
of cells which hate to die, choose to live
in togetherness of growth
sacks on the mill
more on still.

Who will restore the future to a simple room, a summer plain
where mind, not flesh, controls the plan of cities?
Who will level the sudden cancerous mountain?

Had Man No Memory

Had man no memory:
a city without walls
no toll to pay
no promise to keep.
Sleeping, dreaming a safety
waking an honesty;
day devoid of dimness
night of trickery.

In home and street
the warm bread, the cold stone,
the burning, the chill simplicity
of love and hate made one
without boundary

had man no memory.

Photocopier in the English Department

A sound of pumping pumping
the pressure put on
increased
to draw up preserve wine
out of the clay lip
the stone eye
pupiled with fire.

Pupil of fire
photocopier
reproducing fire
at love cost, blood pressure,
wet print the point
of word burst.

The Dreams

My brother kept bantams colored like strawlike copper beech
        leaves;
my sister kept a pet rabbit with a sensitive collapsible nose.
I kept nothing. Nothing stayed with me,
not even snow when I put salt on its glossy white tail
sweeping against the windowpane
with soft floating promises
of obedient captivity,

not even the snail
when I helped it travel a million miles
with one movement of my hand
over dense grass and waste earth
where the robber thistles and highwaymen spiders were lurking,

not even the rescued foreign stamp
when I gave it a family home
a classified accepted understood valued life
on a clean page safe inside a catalogue,
or the dry pressed ragwort
untied with its woolly bear caterpillar in a matchbox.
Nothing stayed.
Dust did not stay, nor shadows. Light,
quietly dissolving the iron bars
sun-melted the key,
splintered the wooden food bowls,

84

set warm with warning
of inevitable prison.

Then one day my brother's bantams with their heads chopped off
ran in a panic up and down the fowl house;
my sister's pet rabbit escaped and did not know
fear of the hawk and ferret.
The bantams, the rabbit died.
Snow remained free, and snails, caterpillars, stamps, dust,
light entering the sky on its own terms.

I was a child then. I turn the memory
while tonight it snows, but I no longer care
for soft promises, and salt is for rubbing into old wounds,
and it is time, while snow still falls, to feed the dreams
that run in panic up and down my sleep
that escape at last and unwittingly make friends with the hawk.

Sunday

Sunday's thermos is filled,
Sunday's hedge clipped, car cleaned, scales played.
The plastic prayer, though it melts in the fire
is contrived in the correct shape
in a lovely contemporary color.

Go fishing in the muddy stream
borrow an inch of beach, rent a sand fly and jellyfish
lie in bed burned bitten and stung
by the lovely contemporary wish
being granted—oh breathless—
on a flesh-colored plastic dish.

Complaint

The motormower a giant wasp on the lawn
reminds me that my nerves are torn.

The TV shots through the wall
do but speak of a Western Hell.

The children's quarrels and cries
tell me where my hate lies.

The traffic changing gear,
the singer without voice or ear,

the loudspeaker from the factory next door,
remind me that I've been here before

in a time quiet enough to hear a thought
parting the tangled stalks of words, creep
soft-footed from the dark into the sure trap
of light, serene light, smooth light;

the splinters piercing the once-quiet spot
remind me that thought without quiet has no shape,
that there's no escape,
that I wish either noise or I were not, were not.

Autumn

The gate to the wood is closed, said Summer.
Take the path over the pond,
kill all the daffodils.
The old men sat wrapped in greaseproof paper,
We are not afraid, they said.
Be shrewd, be whistling.
We are tired of picking locks and seasons.
All things yellow stream down beyond our eyes.

86

Mevagissey Evening

Primroses bright as custard
glossed with rain are dabbed in the hedges
waiting for tomorrow's moderate sun
to switch on, set their blossoming.

At the ned of his last carrion flight
a raven leans against the high wind
as if it were the cenotaph
and he the keeper of the wreaths of light.

Incantations of gulls rise from the sea's mouth;
then gull, raven are quiet; the primroses sleep.
The lonely Silurian rocks, hoisting their story,
sail thorn-labored out of memory.

I Do Not Deny the Sun

I do not deny the sun
that denies me.
I leave the door open,
wheat on the table,
apples in the pantry.
I was warned from the first hour
that the sun did not care,
tearing seasons with his tongue
while maudlin snow ran down his cheeks;
that he snored in a deep white bed
and waking did not as we do
—tell his dreams and embrace callers.

Christmas and Death

Christmas and Death are hungry times
when only the foolish and the dying
with circumscribed vision of Here
learn complete praise, saying
Bravo Bravo to the Invisible.

Who knows to what in the small yard
sunless, the turnkey gives violent praise?
Or the sick man spread
on a white plate in his diminishing world?

Too Cold

When too cold is the room
a memory keeps it warm,
a dropped memory keeps the fire
till Truth robs the meter,
till Time turns off the power.

Memories Again

I have never seen a bedbug, but at night I feel
the irritation of creatures trying to suck my blood.
Sometimes I kill them. In the morning
I see soft squashed memories lying between the sheets.

Three Black Mice

Three black mice with no name,
the equivalent of healthy men in their prime,
sat in a space rocket waiting to be fired.
(Had they been men they might have expired.)

Bred for the occasion—a happy breed,
plugged and wired and battered,
they didn't run after the scientist's wife,
she didn't cut off their tails with the electric carving knife.

No, they died in the sky. See how they fly,
three black mice they fly so high
near the giant paw that cuffs the light,
across ninety million miles of night.

The Footballer in the Small Room

Now he roars through an unlit stadium of silence.
A curve of pain in his head
corresponds to this teamless loneliest game
where his blood has less worth than orange juice,
but the spectator walls do not know his name.

Impard a Willow-Cell in Sordure

Impard a willow-cell in sordure
chance or chead in fascendure
the sweetable clightly photation
frambling in the quintolution.

Chance or chead in vilitance
a musion briskly appleful
harmworthily impelled
in pulse and mind deeprent
with bountiful irrosement.

Graduate

She lives in letters. She knows
the quote, the plot that suits,
the words that fit the moment
as fox gloves fit the fleeing fox
with golden brush and speckled poison
described by him and him and her. Squalid borrower
who dreams another's life, who lives
not under the sun but flat between
another's pages as the useful bookmark, the fringed self-center.

Still she waits for the surprising pool
where nothing grows, no fish have swum before,
no reed or weed has stirred—a hopeless dream
for already·
> —"the sedge is withered from the lake and no birds
> sing."

Rain

The rain runs down the windowpane.
Like.

There's the Great Cliché crying again!

Return

Who spoke of war?
Homecoming is as dangerous as ever.

I'll arm myself.
I'll sit by this pine tree remembering
the purple ice plant, the creeper
(its juice cures the warts of children).

Still the shamrock stems grow to be bitten and sucked,
the periwinkle flower yields honey.

Mr. Universe

The speak-and-run murderer is at large
as his own victim.
In the newspapers and the comic strips
the panic balloons are rising like flares from his lips
in deadly simple navigation to express
his need, his pain and cold:
Help, Ouch, Br-r-r.

He is Mr. Universe of the gonging biceps.
His brute head when the swarm of thought is over wears
the whistling helmet of an empty hive.
And soon, they say, his body as the whipped steed
of cylinders will ride to neigh at the moon
his need his pain and cold
—Help, Ouch, Br-r-r—
in secret hope of an answer.

The Poet

Though the wheat is so beautifully puffed
the rice is ballooned and stuffed
and the world seems so much bigger
from a few to a marvelous crowd
of supers, the pushing and proud
with more push and pride and the prig growing prigger.
The poet still breathes with one lung
climbs a ladder of only one rung
shoots at stars with his hand off the trigger.

Matthew

It is Matthew dressed in sea wave, scarcely walking
for weeds about his ankles, his life willingly
set in the stocks of ocean, pelted with light,
with ripe leaves from inland trees,
grievance of sharp deserted shells.
Open the door to him and the Dog Night.

He will stand there pleading the innocence of salt and cockle
        tooth
though his life has savored many tears from the biting tide.
Over his thin unwashed body, congealed sunlight,
the black and white defiances of grave and shell
defiances of grave and shell
minstrel his passionate reason to be: it is, interpret
all shapes of wave, shell, and gull in flight.

Clairvoyant for what lives and is not human
the black Dog Night at his heels he walks night and day
by this dead sea where, Arabs of summer, children
holidaymaking bring new ancient scrolls to light.

O bandit gull, nomad wave,
from babbling cave of dungeon to articulate man,
man weeping,
man walking upright!

Telephonist

Her sense of humor has no gold stop
or sweetly flowing channel.
Her heavy feet plough tweed
through a silk and lace paddock of earth,
upturning pink daisies and hoppity mice
with no by your leave or remedial poem.

She can laugh with any farmer,
her arms akimbo, her mouth braying
the yokel burden of a woman
who slaps daylight on the back
who walks in her lace country
with every flea-bitten shaggy dog.

Yet for eight hours each day
in the swiveling city of concrete
the talking wire commands her loud mouth.
She becomes the vital link, the braying ass
bearing news of life and death
to the hungry starstruck city.

Gods

Who said Gods have no need to dream?
They dream darkest and most,
their night eyes inflaming a realm
their waking weeps as lost.

Chafing through torture of control
burning mastery, they serve;
sleeping in soul made mortal
embrace their human love.

The lonelier their peaks of cloud
the closer their dreams come
to warm plain and peopled hillside
—Gods most have need to dream.

Overheard

Too cosy stifling sky uncover us,
untwine the veins of scarlet and black wool
worn nearest the ripe skin of our struggle

to keep warm our winter illusion.
Rip off the blanket, unlock the sun,
        sang the elderberry in full juice.

Few words are needed for the distance
the miles between unlocking and going in;
only many desperate speechless years of worn
bleeding knuckles making a battering
bone and hailstone and fire dance on the door,
        sang man from his elderberry house.

The Bittern

I saw a bittern ten yards away. I did not hear him boom.
He was so close you'd have thought he would cry out, tolling
a solitary bell for more Room, Room, Room.

Silence. Neither of us moved. After years of time I knew
he was unafraid. The fear was mine. Unspeaking, menacing
this bogged world, always ten yards away, stands Doom, Doom,
        Doom.

Aunt Winter

What is there for her to do?
She has nothing to keep her fingers busy.
She does not crochet, knit, tat or sew.
Now that is a lonely old age in store. And I?
I have fifteen grandchildren; she is a childless widow.

Three pullovers, one layette, two pairs of gloves.
One matinee coat for the eighteen-month-old;

94

two woolly hats, stockings, cardigans,
the ten-year-old's dress; my winter quota
while her hands have done nothing, nothing but sit on their
        shadows in the sun.

Last year's grass is mown, the leaves have fallen;
nests empty and wet in the forks of the bare trees
say that last year's birds have flown.
If only she had learned to stitch, knit and clothe!
Why should lilies of the field bud
from the shadow of her hands
while I tat and knit to keep the grass and trees decently dressed?

The Dead

I have nothing to say to the dead
unless they approach me first.
It is their right to come to me
with a soft step, singing
or moaning as they please.

The dead cry all night under the trees.
I never tire of listening to them.
Sometimes I want to invite them in
to warm their hands by the fire
but nobody wants the dead inside,
especially not the living. Lock the door,
keep them out, they say,
or the next thing you know
they will overcome you with death,
they will feed from you, rob you,
tap your blood and your preserved memory.
The dead have no memory. A torn scarf
flows in and out of their head, controlled
by the wind of forgetfulness, not by the dead,

and where the end or the beginning may be
the dead do not know
who have no memory, no memory.

As I Walked Along the Street

As I walked along the street I heard
a transistor singing like a bird,
an advertisement from 4ZB
singing in the cherry tree.

I said, So high, so far away
you sing in the push-button sky.
Have you a message of faith and hope?
It said— Use Lily-Clean Soap.

And I was angry then and tried
to forget the transistor bird
but its voice came loud in the world so green
—With Hexachlorophine.

Then I smote the bird and I smote the tree
and the push-button sky fell down on me,
and dying I lay alone without hope
or faith or Lily-Clean Soap.

A Marriage

Cottonwool under the eyelids,
cosmetics on the drained face,
a skillful injection, a sweet-smelling
anointment on the dark turtle belly;
her death has a serene life.

Grind grind in the dark
how hard it is to kill bones!
After the ceremony he goes with his pestle
to do what fire refused—create ashes
to try to prove the dead are dead.

All this preserving, all this burning and proving
leaves him with no power
to stop up the many mouths of the soul
to anoint the swelling darkening memory
to pick out, pestle to ashes, and prove dead
the bones of love lying
indestructible in the fire.

Nouns

This is that
nouns on the mill
more on still
more on still

grind easily but when
you hold the one
worldwide sample of word
of noun and man

take care of it
you can't ungrind
it you will cry
in the mill wanting

the worldwide sun
that once had room
to shine of fields of wheat
on every noun and man.

A Light Verse

Now here's an introduction to
the bear who lives inside the Zoo.
He lived in houses many years,
he was a man with hopes and fears,
he breakfasted on bread and honey,
he worked all week to earn small money,
he was a teacher quite contrary
in a state school secondary
who found one day he'd nothing left
of all material things bereft
including his most faithful wife
who suited him as fork to knife
or knife to fork it doesn't matter
upon the matrimonial platter
which is which, except that she
could cut him more convincingly
with words and ways—that poor young teacher
hacked and hagged in every feature!

He thought it best (as many do)
to go to live inside the Zoo.

Snowdrop

Snowdrop where the slugs chewed
your body in half,
the time has spread oil
your wounds to heal.

You and I will never know
this year's flower. It is
like a lost vision that will swell
to fill all seasons.

I hear the heavy white bell
begin to toll.
I see the sad procession move
towards the white cathedral.
The sun shining on the green spires
is so beautiful.

Another Country

Something the undertakers
do not choose to undertake
is to grow the tree
that provides the wood
for the coffin of man woman and child.

Small white coffins
thin as planks
like chocolate boxes go
down the slopes past the Stations of the Cross.

The sea out there is warm, filled with refuse;
in early morning the fishing boats cough their morning coughs.
The passage of provender is cleared:
God will provide.

Fish, fish,
what is your wish? Silver-shining
and no one can tell if you are dead or not.
You die,
your nerves stay dancing all night
to the lost tune of life.

Church bells toll. It was a child dead,
a marriage, a feast day.
Tomorrow the band will play,
the children twirl their skipping ropes under the eucalyptus trees;
the white dust will rise to cover their faces.

99

Declining the Offer of a Pair of Doves

Chiefly being, they may best be
inside me where is room
for their flying free,
though how much room
I do not know,
I think more than a stone's throw;
a stone will splash in the well,
beneath the well is the fire,
beneath the fire the impossible
keeps warm and doves may also.

They are said to be Peace. Nothing
that feeds is Peace, peck
and get, stab and bleed; would it not
be wiser to have the reputation of a sea gull
and improve slowly?

Thank you. Though I do not accept your doves
I think their twilight color, their shape
stay forever with me; a dove in its shape, anywhere
is free. I who am free
do not know how to borrow
my clothes from the morning and night sky
or the pearl cloud fed by thunder
worn this year next year and forever—
I might know, if I were a dove,
if I were free in my cage and could still fly.

Skid Row No-Hoper

Skid Row No-Hoper
Brandy Blue
what if the world should set fire to you?

What if men
should pluck out your eyes
and women wear them
as beads in a necklace?

Winking winking diamonds
noose for throat
halo for head,
"Quick, remember the dark moat!"

"I know, I know,"
said Brandy Blue
No-Hoper
of Skid Row.

"I remember the dark
immersion
without season
how blind lungless
I was cradled
seaworthy,
my hands crossed
like a twisted mast
before me.

"I remember the dark
secret flag that flew
royally
for Brandy Blue

"and I remember how
my periscope led
to the warm mainland
of flesh and blood

"how I clung, rocked
in the warm wet dark
how I was loved, struck,
cursed and fed."

"Brandy Blue
what will happen to you?"

"An angel will come
at closing time
to lead me home
—such is the usual rhyme;
but I think there will be no one
to wipe up the swill
to clean my vomit away
put gentle words in my mouth
to greet the raging day

"there will be no one
only a welfare worker
who will cover my face with a sheet and say
—It was his blood's chemistry.

"Blood is visible
being is not.
I wish that I had stayed
in the dark moat.

"The ruined castle lies
hollow as dandelion with dock
sunrising through its stones
that were my mother's bones.

"Her eye was a sea
that could swallow me.
In my submarine home I peered above the
surface
through the periscope
and saw the shape of her love
its parallels and crooked lines, triangles
and circles complete . . .

"and saw the strange shape
of her
and saw the inevitable shape
of her dry earthly love

"and I heard her say
one laughing day,
O fish might fly
and she meant me

"for I was a fish
swimming in her wish
in a bowl of flesh
on blood-weed fed

"till time took a hammer
he broke the bowl
and I lay gasping
in the bloody swill

"and no one thought
to put me back.
They flapped each fin
I gasped with shock
and air came in.
I lay defeated
my drowning in air completed."

"O Brandy Blue
what will happen to you?"

"Nothing I know
but tomb is womb
and womb is tomb
and Brandy Blue is my name
Brandy Blue, No-Hoper
of Skid Row."

Janus

A God-like sentry, had focused the past and future,
he smiled double, spied quadruple,
pensioned childhood butterflies,
grew daisies on an old woman's grave.

His gaze divided, forever turning,
he never left or entered the room.
He spied for us. With his charity and rare deformity
he played the private eye observing time,

while we enjoyed the feast. Our tomorrow's table laden
with cherries and wine (our charm of blood against hunger)
we cried gratefully in one breath, "Bring the sentry wine,
bring the sentry wine. He spied for us!"

Yes, he spied for us. We killed him. He deserved his death
who uncovered our past and future crime.

By the Sea

The waterbird
keeps close to the water
its ally in grace

the seal slips through water
curls on the black rock
shelved in sleep lifts
a fin to scratch, wave delicately
fanlike
tough body snub nose plump gray bottom
wrapped in close-knit fur
black snake dancer in the water
snout on the surface
pig eyes
snake body charming dancing

seals huddled on the lonely cape

the water
its ally in grace
salt water
the land lies down with her hair in the water
permanently waved
tugged by the sea
pulled violently
the dancing hair the only part of the land that dances
swept, plaited stroked by the tide
is it grass or seaweed
the long golden grass bleached by the sun

my gratitude for the sea
as provider of grace
is without end

my gratitude for the dream that carried the sea,
unpacked it,
spread it here at our feet.

A Painting by Colin McCahon

During Easter weekend in Dunedin
after the hammer has hammered
and the nails are driven in
my neighbor stands back satisfied
he has made a secure house.

I think there is a wind blowing
through walls, bringing rain
to sealed houses and weatherproof people
and aches into the long propelling bones
the bones that get my neighbor and me and you somewhere;
that grip, run, embrace, reach to take.

Two letters X and P I saw set down
in order, clean and white as bones
upon a neglected earthpage covered with fungus
like gray moss but the propelling letters shone through
and a thumbnail-nicked corner of the sky
while human heads leaned dark against the mountain.

X-Pel, X-Plode, X-Press,
X-Pire, punge and pyre and plain (will you?)
ornate in their loneliness
bearing their shape with pride locked together
Pity and Cross that is kiss, wrong, the lost unknown
the mark that tells the plague flower is within and, blossoming,
will look out the window of
the hammered house made secure,
offering honey.

Summer

1

People work in their gardens
digging raking
hoeing bedmaking
blanketing small plants
that with heads hanging
sulk say I'm thirsty,
give me a drink, more food.
I'm hungry, I want to go home.
Cuffed by wind
washed by night rain
they promise to grow and be good.

Wisteria and clematis
in tethered blue and cream clouds climb
on walls and rotted fences

up and over broken palings
and lilac holds its twilight flame
near the gate or the hedge fronting the street.

It is the time of the slater and the dark-shelled beetle,
the broken bird's egg on the footpath,
the raw dead younker
with enormous mouth
and jewel-sized intestine.

It is the time of the sun
the sun the sun
smiling in the sun the people go
to work and play
believing it was always so
faithfully in the sky.

2

Spring came with my paper-white narcissi.

Now summer is here, it seldom rains,
the ground is cracked open in dry ravines
and wasps fly into the sitting room.
                              Wasps.
I sense their danger, fear their anger.
I flick and whoosh and try to direct them
where the beautiful outside world waits with
enough sky for sable gluttonies of
swarming but pursuing their made-up minds
they argue back at me fuse fuse flame-sting
then sliding surprisedly from sidetrack
to main road they're out from under the tight-
fitting iron house hood on leafy decks
riding the fleeting rapids of light; in
doorways lounging by thinly walled patios
demolished in a season—
                              how can they?

Their made-up minds were right. They should never
have gone out, they should have stayed winter-long
hissing fuse fuse into flame lighting
my windows with their angry glory.

3

Summer. Now the evenings belong
to those under age who stray
and are called home lovingly
by name, to sleep.

The world is dark.
I am out so late. I do not
think it is good for me to be so long awake.
I will stop growing.

My bones will wither and rot,
my face will get sores.
I will stand quietly here. I will listen
for the calling of my name.

I put my ear to the grave.
How busy the dead are
with their eternal furnishings
outlook and future.

Blank faces; thoughts
elsewhere, a calculation
of profitless decay.
And now everyone has gone away.

Come home, come home at once. Come in from out under the
                    night sky!
But there is no one calling my name
and the voice is I,
and my bed is my grave, and to sleep is to die.

Some Thoughts on Bereavement

Loss that in its time caused much mourning
disbelief, bewilderment, crying:

the loss first of the first warm home with
breathing walls, confrontation of air

full of storm and traveling dust, and
no special place again anywhere

not even in death though urn and stone
carry persuasion of tenancy.

The first cry is Everything has changed.
The first glance is backward, the first thought

is compare. The bubble of time need not
enclose me. I will break it and go

where I used to be in familiar
places. And the first shock is loss of

everything as if by fire or bomb
and never again will the loss be so deep.

We hold separate fragile lives.
The shuddering seismic years topple,

home, dreams, people, ideas, all.
My history? I remember loss

of my grandmother, just that she went
away and did not come back for tea.

Of my grandfather who was taken
out of the red front gate with the hand-hole

in it where the latch was and I peeped
through and the hearse was shining black like

the polished marble clock in the dining
room. Of Aunty Maggie who choked on

every cherry stone; it was her throat.
There was no treatment for it. She died.

These are deaths and causes. Bereavement
is after, when people do not come

home for tea and beds are not slept in
and clothes not worn again gather dust.

Bereavement is waiting, waiting for
a known death to be undone, a time

eating itself to excrete the past.
Bereavement is the handling of shreds

that once made a whole garment.
It is seeing in the street a face,

hearing a voice that no one alive
will claim again or show interest in.

Those who are bereaved feel the sense of
waste. For a time they go outside time

and sit crouched in one place with their mouth,
their eyes and their body full of dust.

Though some striking out will say Why Why
and throw the blame like a spear on friends

and family, on world, man and God.
And some turning the spear to their hearts

will almost bleed to death from their guilt
until their rage and grief growing cool

they sit with the triumph of ice and
the patience of stone and wait for love

to shift them and reveal the green life
underneath, for always the bereaved

conceal with their grief new forests, new
generations, bright colors, strong wings.

In loss the trees bear stings, and flowers
carry pain as if it were honey.

The sun is cruel. The daylight does not
understand or why does it not bring

back the dead? And God is only a
desperately personified mood

of man in his need. Grief becomes spread
like arsenic upon the warm new

bread of living: it is the slow
working of the last poison of life:

I love. In dying I kill. Such is
the law of some insects and all men.

People, animals died. Known, unknown.
Cats with wet stiff fur. Dogs that were put

to sleep in gas chambers and never
seen again. A bloated dead horse we used

to watch peeing with his immense thing
but did not really know or love. The

maggots whispered like pine trees inside
his cavernous belly, and he stank.

But these again are deaths. Absence is
the chief pain, wanting the death undone,

and when this dream is killed, the mourning
is for the dream and not for the dead

and then because dreams are within, it
is not important to move or speak

or eat, only to coffin-cradle
the lost dream in mourning without hope.

Sisters, parents . . . many known have died
but these are not the worst hammer blows.

We are literate in death. We learn
early the grammar, the subtleties,

vocabulary of the language;
and grief and loss are every day our

faithless teachers. We have learned that men
living may be translated as dead,

that the known dead may yet be alive.
Feeling death in a gesture, a glance,

a word spoken, we proceed to mourn
and often do not know what we mourn

or where it has gone, for burial
of love does not require stone or urn

and is its own pretence; and death of
a moment may never be confined

not even in memory but—O!
with all longing and tears may be mourned!

Loss is bewilderment, loneliness,
a vanished moment, an idea,

someone loved, maybe not even loved,
but all things once near, lost forever,

in death that uproots the familiar world
we shelter under and feed on. It

is hard to plant again with salt rain
in darkness and without hope of sun.

The Ancient Mother, a Shape of Pumice

Her precious load has dropped in her belly.
If she stays here squatting on my desk calendar
I shall have to act as midwife to her.

Her body is gray
as spring-cleaned evil or shop-soiled good.
She was burned at white heat in the volcanic fire
and now her riddled bones are set
while her body in its swollen shape submits for ever
to the black-masked highwayman calendar:

I will stand, I was born to stand here patiently.
It is you, and you, and you who must deliver.

Once, Between Myself and the Pine Trees

Once, between myself and the pine trees on the hill
thoughts passed, like presents. Unwrapping them I found
common words that I, not trees, knew and could afford:
lonely, sigh, night. The pines had given me
my seven-year self but still kept their own meaning in the sky.

Now, in exchange of dreams with a remoter world
I still unwrap, identify the presents;
and always tired recognition gives way to hope
that soon I may find a new, a birthday shape,
a separate essence yielded without threat or deceit,
a truthful vocabulary of what is and is not.

The Bure

It is places that will not perish. I think
this now—tomorrow I may have changed my mind,
found other ways of apportioning death
between man and the earth he walks on.

I hold the Bure rising in its first
mist of water, a beginning breath
of air, unlearned in the art of flowing
though two swans try to teach it who floats there.

Earth teaches it, makes its bed
beneath with weeds and stones
while the marsh orchids desperately need
its dim mirror to repair their freckles.

Confident, it surges by the mill
swirls under the brige, widening
to the wherry-drifting reed-bordered
water where people drown in summer.

Today the Bure rises in my head;
stays, while people drown, though bones,
lost years ago, still give up
memories and the recently dead

hold sodden dreams in every pocket.
Today I have only the Bure, the mysterious
marsh of its beginning, that wild wind blowing
from Denmark through Cromer and the North.

Blickling Hall. The Lake. Flint Cottages.
Mountains of sugarbeet and steaming manure;
wheat and barley fields; an aluminium
sky blackened at its high edges by storm.

I hold these today in their first mist rising
across the marsh of memory
where people and places will drown; only, today
the Bure, the orchids, the two floating swans will stay.

Letter

Dear friend, the here–there emphasis is made
to keep you at a distance as I write,
to fix you, no captured human specimen
in a crowded corner of a northern world
reminding only how with spear, nail, pen,
I came your way walking from paddock to field
until at noon I feel asleep in an oak tree's shade
and waking saw not manuka and the Southern Cross
but above, Orion, and at my feet, lady-white.

A skin-thin air letter, a ninepenny stamp:
(rata or manuka or koromiko)
or words on a yellow pink green or white page
are the plan I must make, the obstacles overcome
before the public service and the plane take over my rage
to speak to you, speed-shrivel the ten thousand miles to your home
in the Midlands—fire and blotting-paper damp,
spring-feverishly mourning always the sky's loss
of sun, hanging out to dry bones stained with snow,

gray snow, last winter's fall. What else have I learned
of your city since I traced the millions
crowded on a sinking full-stop as on a doomed raft
in my first geography book and read its important name
and meaning? Small arms, bicycles, heavy drift
of smoke upward all day; diesel fumes, oil-flame, then, cultural
            flame
from science and music where some, not all, once burned,
survived by grafting new tissue to others who, wary at first,
soon strutted proud and warm in their smart new skin.

Meat markets, medicine, city dignitaries; an electrified line
to London from Central Station or Snow Hill.
Edgbaston. Selly Oak. A Chamberlain in office.
A Bull-Ring. Art Gallery. Dustmen. Council Flats.

Association on Association of men in business.
Undertakers, clerks, brokers; with umbrellas and top or bowler
        hats.
And tarnished incomes and incomes that when polished, shine.
A city of reservoirs of resigned fluoridic thirst
suckling the sweet channels flowing from the Welsh Hills.

Men silent in trains who'd never dare risk
the five-pound fine by pulling the communication cord.
Men with scientific journals; dark eyes
seeing molecules as fellow passengers
or, seeing women, tricking intelligence to tell where lies
the difference as both wrapped in genetic furs
deceive yet are worth study as a lifetime's task.
You'd think I talk of any city, not only Birmingham—
but where else into the mould are men women and bicycles
        poured

with equal reverence? Wheels within wheels
headlights reflectors handlebars
pumps pedals carriers hand and foot brakes,
oh and not to forget the rifles, the agricultural machines,
the bath and the kitchen sink; the articles Birmingham makes
would equip you from birth to death and after—here the touching
        scene
could be looked at, not through your eyes, but through locally
        made cinema reels,
as taking in the used label of your life, *Tear Round Here. I Am.*
You replace it with *Snip, Cover and Fold. I Was.*

My geography book is out of date. Following the new
recognition of humanity by humanity,
the miles of mountain chains everywhere
(you remember their paralyzed snowcapped vertebrae)
have been made free, while rivers too have claimed their share
in the new deal, have changed their flow and no longer obey
the command of the geography book I once knew.

And now Birmingham, to me, is famous not for bicycles but for
      people.
It is the heart profits when facts are produced in an enlightened
      factory.

But it's no use. You are not there. The essence of your being
is you flow, lap at far coasts, enter rooms
invisibly to reassure me when I'm afraid
though it's not to be interpreted that therefore
I worship you, regard you as my private God.
When you're an old man you'll have a face like an apple in store,
a corner apple smelling of rain and wood, seeing
through narrow eyes nails taller than any steeple,
dead leaves and spiders set beside white scientific glooms

—does this image of you seem strange? You'll allow
it's not the usual glimpse of God; it's worse—
a theft of a separate being to complete a torn memory;
a slave-selection more frightening, tyrannical,
than is made in any past or present book of geography;
a callup of a memory-guard I've no right to call.
Death is the only guard who's willing and free Here and Now
to stay at my door, to play the memory game,
to plead too often—A bicycle? Had you not better choose a hearse?

Personal Effects

A torn plastic wallet containing a fishhook,
a rusted screw, a lucky piskie from Cornwall,
folded tattered notices of my first book,
holiday snaps of children now twice as tall
or dead, a silver watch with a broken face
marked Shockproof, though not the watch the little Levite
kept, in the hymn, in the hished evening place
of dark temple courts and dim lamplight . . .

though my father's name was Samuel. Which ear must I have,
and why, I used to wonder, to hear the Word?
. . . a bright half-inch nail . . . a letter from a new love,
a tarnished bluebird brooch my mother had.
Then, as if to lure this dreary flotsam from his last high tide,
beautiful wave-skimming Greenwell's Glory, my father's pride.

Christmas

In my country Christmas is
frangipanni
jacaranda
pohutukawa

is the flotsam holiday court in residence;
the king of the golden river
in swimming trunks, rubbed with sun oil,
saving the stupid who would drown outside the flags.

In my country Christmas is sun
is riches that never were rags
is plenty on the plate
is nothing for hunger who came unseen

too soon or too late;
is holiday blossom beach sea
is from me to you
is from you to me

is giving giving
in a torture of anxiety
panic of pohutukawa
jacaranda that has lost all joy.

In my country the feast
of Christmas is free;
we pay our highest price
for the lost joy
of the jacaranda tree.

L-Driver

An L-Driver through poetry,
he swerved to avoid a homily
and struck a metaphor; nothing
could save it; he drove on in shame
leaving no address and a false name.

And now his obsession is
the miraculous escape; he asks, what if
I swerve again, but having no murdered metaphor
to support me I plunge to my death over the cliff?

In a Garnet World

In a garnet world
something troubles the rock
—a rash, an itching dazzle
that will not sleep or be soothed,
a night sky of stars without sky
or night; and stars that sting.

This rock once unseen
in its river of ice, is now sick.
A man climbing cloud-high
caught human sight of it
brought to it this blood-colored incurable
infection of light.

Unemployment

Each Tuesday at ten o'clock I go to the Employment Exchange,
fill in the form they give me, tell what I have earned
for chopping down the neighbor's tree, feeding his horse,
rescuing a silly sheep from the swamp. Sometimes, with odd jobs,
I make as much as a pound a week, but no one
offers anything permanent. The official (whom I knew at school,
a bear in the back seat) gapes at me: I'm sorry we cannot place
      you.
And therefore I am not placed, not in this or that. I have
a fine box of tools that I keep well-oiled. I have experience
and knowledge tied in a waiting bundle in the corner of my mind
nearest the door but no one knocks and the door is never opened.

I collect my weekly allowance. I go home,
I cuddle my wife, feed the cat,
and, for no purpose in no place, grow fat.

The Foxes

Within the purple graph of the Hokonuis, the dark
peak of Milford, my memory of Wyndham is drawn to scale.
I see the weathered gray sheep pens, their gates askew,
still standing not used now, scattered with old sheep dirt
like shriveled berries of a deadly nightshade
that lead me to suppose a spreading sheep tree grew here.
I cannot remember. The widest tree was the sky. Also,
deadly nightshade is poisonous, and sheep are not, are they?

The trains used to pass here. Wyndham station is closed now
and the railway lines like iron thorns are lifted
from their sleeper beds. The stranded station hangs
a sheltering verandah over no human traveler

for the track is overgrown with grass and it is grass, rooted on
   the platform,
stay-at-home, that meets only the wind passing through
with hospitality of plaintive moan and sigh
instead of the usual cup of tea and meat pie.

Sunday and topdressed the spring hills prosper with grass
the home paddocks with plump ewes and night-mushrooming
lambs, pink underneath, proudly declared
in the national interest, edible. The sheep, like subsidized legends,
   thrive,
their keepers too, but my childhood Wyndham has stayed
secure in its mutinous dream, unchanged since I knew
the railway house by the railway line and was five,
starting school, walking through long grass where the foxes lived.